How to Teach Reading and Spelling

Bringing the Science of Reading into the Classroom

Sasha Borenstein

How to Teach Reading and Spelling

Bringing the Science of Reading into the Classroom

by Sasha Borenstein

© 2021 Sasha Borenstein

Published by Science of Reading Press, Ashland, Oregon.

Cover & Book Design: Chris Molé, booksavvystudio.com

Library of Congress Control Number: 2020926036

ISBN: 978-1-7363087-0-7

First Edition

Printed in the United States of America

Dedicated to all of the students and teachers
I have had the privilege to work with and learn from.

Table of Contents

PART IV: Reading and Spelling Long Words - Multi-Syllable Skills

Syllable Lessons

Morphology

References and Resources

Appendices

About the Author

SASHA BORENSTEIN has worked in the fields of Special Education and literacy for fifty years as a classroom teacher, remediation specialist, diagnostician, college instructor, and educational consultant. Sasha received undergraduate training at UCLA in Psychology and Special Education, after which she completed her graduate work in Special Education at Columbia University, Teachers' College.

In 1977, Sasha founded The Kelter Center, a private remediation clinic in Los Angeles, California, where she was the director for thirty-six years. In addition to teaching students, she trained, mentored, and supervised other teachers in their work with children and adults with learning disabilities and dyslexia. During this period, she also served as a consultant, trainer, and mentor with many educational establishments in Los Angeles, Santa Monica, Malibu, Culver City, Long Beach, Oak Park, and the Manhattan Beach Unified School Districts.

Sasha's work with private and charter schools included Pressman Hebrew Academy, El Jardin de Las Familias, Camino Nuevo Charter School, Synergy Charter School, Summit View School, Landmark West School, The Dunn School, and Charles Armstrong School. In addition, she created classes and remedial programs for medical students at Drew University of Science and Medicine, and has been a presenter for the International Dyslexia Association, the California Association of Resource Specialists, the Bureau of Jewish Education, and the Learning Disabilities Association.

The overarching principle throughout Sasha's career has been to understand and translate rigorous educational research into classroom practices. Programs she has worked with extensively include: *The LiPs Program (2003), Educational Care: A System for Understanding and Helping Children with Learning Problems at Home and in School,* Mel Levine (2013), *Step Up to Writing,* Maureen Aumann (2008), *A Taxonomy of Learning, Teaching and Assessing; A Revision of Bloom's Taxonomy of Educational Objective (2001),* and *Unlocking Literacy,* Marcia Henry (2011).

Sasha, who currently lives in Oregon, doesn't seem to know how to stop teaching. She is in private practice serving individual students, while training classroom teachers in several schools. She has written this book to help both teachers and parents in guiding children, adolescents, and adults to become thoughtful, engaged readers and spellers.

Part I

Introduction

Introduction

Why Teach Reading and Spelling Explicitly?

I N THE FIELD OF READING AND SPELLING RESEARCH and the translation of that research into classroom practice, there are many superstars: Louise Moats, *Teaching Reading is Rocket Science*, Mark Seidenberg, *Language at the Speed of Sight,* Farrell's explanation of *The Simple View of Reading*, Scarborough's *Reading Rope*, David Kilpatrick, *Equipped for Reading Success;* and Spear-Swerling's discussion of *Structured Literacy*. These people and many others have participated in the extensive research that has been conducted for decades in the arena of literacy which has provided us with answers of *what* to teach.

We know that given strong teacher preparation and support, 95% of all students can be taught to read and spell. The National Assessment of Educational Progress provides insight into the fact that many students are unable to read, spell, or comprehend what they are reading, and others cannot use writing skills adeptly to express their thinking.

All students, no matter their age, socio-economic status, or ability to learn will benefit from being taught to read and spell in a conscious, explicit, organized manner.

Many teachers feel at a loss when faced with reading and spelling lessons because the rules and regularities, as well as the exceptions to the rules, can be quite overwhelming. When students ask why words are spelled a certain way, don't understand concepts their teachers are trying to convey to them, or make mistakes, the teacher's manual does not contain anything to assist in addressing these challenges. All too often teacher training doesn't cover knowledge about our language either.

Thus, the purpose of this book is to actively guide teachers, educational therapists, tutors, and parents through the process of helping students acquire the linguistic concepts that are the bedrock of learning to read and spell. The study of *phonology* (sounds that make up the English lexicon), *orthography* (spelling patterns), *morphology* (meanings of prefixes, suffixes, and root syllables), and *etymology* (the origins of English words) can be taught carefully and clearly to help learners become actively involved in learning the English spelling and reading system.

The lessons in this book have been crafted to provide educators with words that exemplify each concept to be taught, questions to ask to encourage students to actively think, and activities which will help students understand the logic and elegance of how to spell and read words thoughtfully. In addition, considerable discussion will be devoted to learning how to correct mistakes in order to develop self-correcting thinking processes in your students.

Structured Literacy

Structured Literacy is a meeting of research and classroom teaching approaches that is highly effective in teaching all students to read and spell thoughtfully delineating how to teach carefully and clearly by:

1. Following a clear, thoughtfully orchestrated sequence of literacy skills while directly teaching letters and their sounds, syllable types and morphemes, as well as vocabulary.

2. Cycling back and forth, reviewing learned skills frequently.

3. Maintaining a dialogue between teacher and students.

4. Using carefully selected examples and non-examples while teaching.

5. Having students practice what they learn by reading decodable texts.

6. Providing prompt, precise feedback to students.

Spear-Swerling, 2018

Let's now define some of the key terms used in Structured Literacy. Lessons where you will learn how to implement these ideas are referenced after each definition.

Explicit means concepts are taught clearly and directly by the teacher because students should not be expected to infer them simply from exposure or incidental learning (Archer & Hughes, 2011). The Teacher Student Dialogues in each lesson provide clear, student-friendly definitions and dialogues to teach every concept.

Systematic and sequential means that skills and concepts are taught in a logical order, with important, prerequisite skills taught first (Torgesen, 2006). The order of lessons in this book is based upon the structure and history of the English language, with Anglo-Saxon consonants and vowels taught in Section II followed by one-syllable spelling patterns in Section III. In Section IV Anglo-Saxon syllable types are presented, as well as Anglo-Saxon inflectional and derivational suffixes. These lessons are followed by Latin prefixes, suffixes, and root syllables, as well as Greek combining forms.

Cumulative practice and ongoing review of previously learned skills ensure that students will retain these skills and develop automaticity. A regular check on how much students have retained over time is essential and should take place on a recurring basis. Creating a record keeping document that is filled out for each student or group of students, so previously taught concepts can be reviewed and readily recalled is an excellent way to accomplish this. A copy of that kind of document appearing in Appendix A can be added to or rearranged based upon your literacy scope and sequence.

Each lesson should incorporate review activities and games designed to practice three, four, or five different spelling patterns. Spelling rules written on cards to be used during these games may be shuffled through randomly while students are asked to name several words that exemplify the rule on the card. Spelling quizzes afford opportunities to evaluate students' knowledge of spelling patterns and provide feedback about their work. In each lesson, games and word lists—as well as other published resources—are provided.

A high degree of student-teacher interaction means that considerable time be spent in direct teaching (Archer & Hughes, 2011). With dialogue as the heart of each lesson, instructors are given simple, direct, relevant questions to use so students can think about words and ideas while developing hypotheses and testing out these ideas. Students must be actively involved in the learning experiences by answering questions, sorting words, explaining their thinking aloud, summarizing concepts, and self-evaluating to demonstrate their acquisition of the information taught.

Teaching that includes carefully chosen examples and non-examples emphasizes and promotes active learning. Each lesson provides specific examples and non-examples of words that illustrate the reading and spelling principle taught in that lesson.

Because the English language has "many exemplary regularities" (Perfetti, 2003), the lessons in this book guide teachers through a specific sequence in order to teach the regular patterns inherent in the consonant letter/sound relationships of single and multi-syllable patterns. Kearns and Whaley add the sage advice to "Teach the simplest, consistent patterns, and hide the rest" until the students build stamina and confidence in thinking about reading and spelling words (Kearns & Whaley, 2019).

Decodable texts are stories and articles that have a minimal number of words that have not been explicitly taught to the learner. One of the leading organizations in the United States supporting and training teachers with Structured Literacy practices is The Reading League. All of its publications are valuable resources for literacy teachers. See Appendix F for a list of decodable texts to use with students of all ages recently compiled by the Reading League.

Prompt and corrective feedback directs the teacher to use feedback that teaches students to self-correct. If a student makes a mistake in the course of their work, guiding them with corrective feedback will build their self-correction skills.

Initially, the teacher must evaluate the mistake the student makes by asking themselves why the student would give that answer, what he or she is possibly thinking, and what might be *correct* about the mistake that the student has made.

In the next step the teacher enters a dialogue with the student, asking her to explain her answer and her thinking process—essentially to "think aloud". Indeed, she may actually have been thinking of something entirely different than what the teacher imagined. Giving the student specific feedback about what was correct in her answer, re-teaching the missing or misconstrued concept, and finally crafting a question with alternate answers so the student can correct her mistake provides a framework for the student to learn how to self-correct going forward. Here is an example of such an interaction:

The teacher asks Sally to spell the word *cake*, and she writes *kake*:

- The teacher postulates that Sally doesn't remember the "c" rule.
- The teacher gives Sally information about all the right sounds in the word and

that the letters are in the correct order in the word she spelled.

- The teacher then asks Sally what spelling rules she applied to this word.
- Sally might reply that because there was a "k" at the end of this word, she would use a "k" for the for beginning sound and that the vowel is a Vowel plus E.

This dialogue alerts the teacher to the fact that she needs to re-teach the C rule and ask Sally how that pattern applies to this word:

- There are two ways to spell the /k/ sound in the beginning of a word "c" and "k," with the most frequent way to spell the /k/ sound being with a "c" if the vowel is not "i, e, or y".
- When asked, "What are the vowels in this word?" Sally answers "a" and "e".
- "Given those vowels, what is the most probable way to spell the /k/ sound in the beginning of the word *cake*, "c" or "k"?
- The answer is "c".

Formative assessment, which means monitoring student's assimilation of new information, can be done in many productive ways. You can ask students to explain concepts in their own words, to give examples of the concepts you are teaching, or have them use a spelling rule during a game. An explanation of the reason for their choice, rather than just answering a question or filling in a blank will tell you more about what is going on in their heads. Creating a rule book in which they can write the definition for a new rule is another useful strategy for ascertaining what the student has understood and what they may be confusing.

Reading and Spelling are Reciprocal

In the article *How Spelling Supports Reading*, Louisa Moats (2005) notes that spelling and reading build and rely on the same mental representation of a word. Knowing the spelling of a word makes the representation of it sturdy and accessible for fluent reading.

Each lesson in this book honors the reciprocating nature of reading and spelling. Students begin by reading the words in each lesson and then spelling those words.

Skill Sequences are Based Upon How the English Language Evolved

The historical development of Modern English provides guidelines for what we must teach our students and in which sequence. English is a polyglot and as such is filled with words from many other languages that add to its beauty and richness. Synonyms from Anglo-Saxon, Latin, and Greek origins abound; *ask, question, interrogate; end, finish, conclude; help, aid, assist.*

Few students are exposed to the story of the evolution of English until they are in high school or college, and yet many words in elementary texts come from each of these different languages. The richness of these ideas can tantalize and excite the budding linguist while aiding in the development of a love of spelling and reading that is too often absent.

Historically, the development of English was based upon wars and conquests, but a thirst among English speakers for variety and spice in their language was also present. The first inhabitants of England were the Celts, who did not have a written language, which is why most of the words they used have been lost to us, although a few, like *avon*, their word for river, remain.

Over time, Germanic tribes known as the Angles, the Saxons, and the Jutes invaded the land of the Celts. These fierce tribes who spoke a one- and two-syllable language gave us some of the most common and basic words in Modern English— *cow, dog, man, woman, child, boy, mother, feed, farm, brown, have, grief, night, rabbit, grumble, table,* and *love*—which are all Anglo-Saxon words.

Many of these words have spelling patterns that are challenging for learners because the letters don't appear to correspond with the sounds that we pronounce. This is often because the scribes who first wrote down the Anglo-Saxon language, and later people who wrote dictionaries, did not always agree on how words were to be spelled.

To give students a flavor for how English used to sound, you can find YouTube videos of people reciting the introduction to Chaucer's *Canterbury Tales* or Shakespeare's plays, which illustrate how Germanic Early and Middle English once sounded.

As English evolved, the pronunciation of many consonants shifted. The "k" in *knight* and the "gh" in *night*, became silent. Another reason for discrepancies in the pronunciation of English words and their spelling is that the sounds of vowels have also changed. The Great Vowel Shift occurred between 1500 and 1650 A.D., during the transition from Middle to Modern English. This was a period when the pronunciation of many words changed, although spelling patterns did not.

Anglo-Saxon English words are built with single consonants, consonant blends, single vowels, vowels plus E, R-controlled vowels, and some vowel digraphs and diphthongs. Words of Anglo-Saxon origin also utilized all of the basic syllable types and created compound words to describe things in the environment like *earrings, outlaw, toenail, fishhook.* To form longer words, prefixes that were prepositions—*by*stander, *under*stand, *in*side, *in*to—were affixed to words. These Anglo-Saxon prefixes and root syllables can stand alone as separate words, unlike Latin prefixes, root syllables, and suffixes, which cannot be separated.

In the year 1066 A.D., the Norman French people, whose language was a mixture of French, Latin, and some German influences, invaded England. The words that English inherited from these languages which are more formal and technical and are used to this day in schools, literature, and textbooks.

Words of Latin origin, which are made up of base or root syllables, contain prefixes and/or suffixes that signal meaning and grammatical categories.

Two English words with Latin origins are:

- **Dentist,** with the suffix *-ist* alerting readers to the fact that this word describes a person, and the root syllable *-dent* which means this is a person who works with teeth.

- **Legislature**, with the suffix *-ture* defining the word as a noun, and the root syllable *leg* which tells us this noun pertains to laws.

The Norman French brought many words to the English language; *country, duke, duchess, court, judge, jury, angel, savior, abbey* and *architecture.*

English spelling and reading patterns are further complicated because the spelling of the words from different donor languages often are retained. Examples of this include *spaghetti, sushi, boutique,* and *beaux* (Kearns & Whaley, 2019). Exploring these words by looking up their etymological origins and the shifts of pronunciation and meaning over time can be interesting investigations to have with your students. This word study can also exponentially expand vocabulary skills, as well as spelling and reading skills.

Knowing one root syllable, then adding different prefixes and suffixes, can be helpful in furthering an understanding of morpheme families. The words *flex, flexible, genuflect, reflector, reflex,* and *reflect* have a common root syllable, and discovering how their meanings are related can be an interesting learning adventure for students.

English words derived from Latin use the same consonant and vowel letters as Anglo-Saxon words, with the exception being an absence of consonant and vowel digraphs. Anglo-Saxon syllable types are present in words of Latin origin, although here they have an additional feature of varied stress patterns that change meaning, part of speech, and pronunciation.

Project can be pronounced with the first syllable emphasized or accented when it is a noun. However, if the second syllable is emphasized or accented, this word becomes a verb. With the word *pagan*, the first syllable receives the emphasis, and the vowel sounds like /ae/, the sound a single vowel usually represents in an open syllable. However, the "a" in the second, unaccented syllable sounds like /u/, the muffled *schwa* sound, not the expected sound of a single vowel, in a closed syllable.

French words also entered the English language. A person who has *courage* has a strong heart, while the *-ique* ending syllable signals a word of French origin in *boutique, antique* and *mystique.* Words like *restaurant, parachute* and *rouge* also come from the French language.

English words of Greek origin have a distinct structure. Instead of having prefixes, root syllables, and suffixes, Greek words use two root syllables with a connective vowel ("o," "u," "i") between the root syllable and the suffix, as in *matriarch, archivist,* and *bibliographer.* Each part of a word of Greek origin, such as *photography* or *dermatology,* has a meaning: *photo-* means light, *-graph* means written or drawn, *-ology* means the study of, and *derma-* means skin.

Words of Greek origin use the same consonants, vowels, and syllable patterns as Anglo-Saxon and Latin words, although a few new letters and sounds are added to words of Greek origin: "ph" says /f/, "ch" says /k/, and "y" says /i/.

All of these ideas about word origins are interesting, but the critical questions for us as educators include:

- How do we introduce these concepts to our students?
- When do we introduce them?
- How quickly do we present the various ideas?
- How many review experiences does each group of students need?

One possible starting point for a study of word origins (*etymology*) can be introduced when students begin to learn the vowels and consonants, which is a natural time to talk about Anglo-Saxon letters, words and spelling patterns, and compound words. When teaching spelling patterns, common Anglo-Saxon suffixes such as the past tense markers, "-ed", plurals "-s", and "-es", possessives, the inflectional ending "-ing," "-ly," "-ness," or "-able", as well as the adjectival comparatives "-er" and "-est" should be taught to all elementary school students (King, 2000, Henry, 2003).

After the teaching of syllable types would be an appropriate time to introduce the concepts of prefixes, suffixes, and roots of Latin and Greek origin. Many books have lists of Latin prefixes, suffixes, and roots with activities designed to practice spelling, reading, and using the resultant words in meaningful ways.

The same is true of the Greek combining forms, with the most important factor being a continuous exploration of the concepts while at the same time building morpheme families and applying these skills to reading and writing of meaningful information.

It is important to remember, however, that the number of ideas and the speed of presentation will be entirely dependent upon the student's absorption of these concepts in relation to their reading, writing, and other schoolwork—which are the touchstones used to gauge student progress. If a student cannot explain the concepts and use them, they have not yet mastered the information, and the pace of teaching this information is moving too quickly.

Lessons in all sections of this book emphasize these ideas about how the English language has evolved over time. Specific lessons teach the Anglo-Saxon letters and sounds, common ways of spelling and syllable types, as well as prefixes, suffixes, and base and root syllables. Concepts and spelling and reading patterns from Latin, Greek, and French source languages are included in Section IV.

	PHONOLOGY		ORTHOGRAPHY	MORPHOLOGY		
A N G L O / S A X O N	**VOWELS** Single Digraphs Dipthongs **CONSONANTS** Single Digraphs Blends	**SYLLABLES** Open Closed Vowel +E R-Controlled Vowel teams Consonant LE	**POSITION** **Protection** **Both**	**COMPOUND WORDS**		
				Prefix be- over- under-	Root + ROOT +	Suffix -ed, -s, -es -er, -est, -ing -less, -ful, -ship
L A T I N	Schwa	Closed Vowel +E R-controlled		Prefix re- sub- il-, in-, im-	Root vent + duct + struct	Suffix -tion, -sion -ous, -ious, -cious -al, -ial
G R E E K	ph/f/ ch/k/ ps/s/ mn/n/ y/i/	Open Closed		Prefix tele- auto- bio-	Root scop crat	Suffix -ic -ic -logy

Concepts That Govern Reading/Spelling Patterns

A study done by Hanna, Hodges, Hanna and Rudorf in 1966 provides educators many gifts about what and how to teach English reading and spelling. This team of researchers chose 17,000 of the most frequently used words in the English language, then asked a computer to sort them based upon the letters and their sounds. What they found was a high degree of consistency, especially with the consonants, and they noted fifty-two speech sounds. They also asked the computer to sort those speech sounds based upon where the sounds occurred in each word, at the beginning, middle, or end of the word or syllable.

These researchers discovered that the computer could predict twenty of these fifty-two phonemes accurately in ninety percent of the words, while another ten phonemes could be predicted eighty percent of the time. Vowels, however, were found to be more variable in their spelling. Eight of the fifty-two phonemes were predictable no less than seventy-eight percent of the time, with five of these eight being vowels. The value of this analysis is that they confirmed a high degree of predictability in the position of sound/letter associations in English.

Another finding was that if the computer was programmed to take into consideration where sounds occurred in words, it could spell fifty percent of the 17,000 words with no errors, and another thirty-six percent of the words with only one error. Ten percent of these frequently used words were considered irregular, and if the computer was programmed to take into consideration a word's origin and meaning, eight percent of those errors could be corrected. The remaining four percent of the classified words that stumped the computer included those which:

- End in the letter "v"—in English a word can never end without "v" being followed by an "e" (*love, live, dove*).
- Contain "-old," "-ild," "-ind," and "-ost" and thus have odd spelling patterns.
- Are high frequency Anglo-Saxon words or were adopted from other languages, and were once pronounced differently.

(Moats, 2000; Hanna, et. al., 1966)

If we teach these patterns and concepts over time to students, they will be able to actively think and problem solve about spelling and reading, rather than having to memorize every word they encounter. They will also learn to love thinking about and exploring how reading and spelling of individual words works because as humans we are inherently problem solvers and adventurers.

Gifts from Hanna et al

Let's look at the findings and the the gifts of Hanna, et al. (1966) and translate them into concepts and teaching strategies that teachers can use.

Gift I

The study lists the frequencies of different spelling patterns in the 17,000 words explored, which is helpful because it suggests both the spelling patterns that will open up the most words for our students, as well as those that are less useful. The quantitative analysis of some spelling patterns will highlight this point.

C pattern: 5,731 words (*cent, corn, cymbal, cycle*)
Vowel plus E pattern: 3,954 words (*base, while, cope, use, beet*)
R controlled vowel pattern: 3,219 words (*bird, fur, better, horn, sharp*)
G pattern: 2,511 words (*get, gym, ginger, gore, gentle*)

Syllable Types

Closed syllable pattern: 10,093 words (*muffin, helpful, comment*)
Open syllable pattern: 3,044 words (*iris, oval, final, orzo*)

Versus:

wo words = 28 words (*word, worth, world*)
tch = /ch/ 63 words (*catch, porch, stretch*)
x = /gz/ 43 words (*exist, exit*)

Emphasizing the patterns that will help our students read and spell the most words is a priority. Introducing these concepts leads to an appreciation that English is a highly predictable, structured language, and knowing these patterns can help students to read and spell more efficiently. In contrast, the infrequent spelling patterns are best taught using mnemonic strategies and mapping strategies.

Gift II

Another way of interpreting the Hanna, et al. (1996) data is to note the most common spellings of vowel sounds. The most common and reliable spellings of vowel sounds are the one letter vowels, the single vowels. Other vowels, digraphs and diphthongs, are spelled with two letters. Knowing the relative frequencies of vowel spelling patterns illuminates which spelling patterns should be taught first, and which patterns should be slowly introduced as alternate spellings.

Long "a" spellings:	Long "o" spellings:
"a-e" = 80% of words	"o-e" = 72% of words
"ai" = 9% of words	"oa" = 5% of words
"ay" = 6% of words	"ow" = 5% of words

Gift III

The research data also furnishes a timeline within which a student should learn different concepts of spelling. When teaching the sounds and positions of the letter "y" within a word, there are four possible choices, and each position in the word determines the sound of the "y" as well as whether or not the letter "y" is functioning as a consonant or a vowel:

- If "y" appears at the beginning of a word, it functions as a consonant and its sound is /ee/. This sound letter correspondence occurred 57 times in the study.

- If "y" is in the middle of a closed syllable, the corresponding sound is /i/, which occurred 162 times in the study. Most of the words with this pattern are of Greek origin.

- If "y" comes at the end of a one-syllable word, it represents the sound /ie/, which occurred 128 times in the study.

- If "y" occurred at the end of a two-syllable word, the corresponding sound is /ee/, and this occurred 1628 times in the study.

When teaching a young child, focus on spelling with "y" at the end of a word and the beginning of a word because a number of common words begin with the letter "y" (*yes, yarn, yard)*. However, when teaching middle school or high school students, teach them *all* of the possible ways to use the letter "y".

Gift IV

The study also explored the positional attributes of orthography. In this book, this concept is called the Position Principle, and it has the following two aspects:

The position of a letter/grapheme within a word determines its sound and spelling.

1. At the beginning of a word "x" sounds like /z/ (*xenon*).

2. In the middle of a word "x" sounds like /ks/ or /gz/ (*excuse, exit*).

3. At the end of a word "x" sounds like /ks/ (*fox, lax, fax*).

The letters that follow a given letter influence the sound of the initial letter, with these influential letters known as "markers".

1. When "c" is followed by the letter "i," "e," or "y," it always sounds like /s/ (cinder, cent, cyst).

2. When "c" is followed by any other letter, it always sounds like /k/ (came, cot, cure, clear, cream).

Gift V

Hanna et al. (1996) also described the relationship between vowels and the orthographic patterns at the ends of words, labeled the Protection Principle in this book. **The sound of a single vowel is easily changed by another vowel or consonant that follows the initial vowel.** The sounds of the vowels in these word pairs illustrate this idea:

can – cane *pal – pail*

con – corn *sand – sang*

If one wants to avoid changing the vowel sound, two consonants must follow the single vowel to protect, or retain its sound. Many spelling patterns protect a weak, one-letter vowel by placing more than one consonant between vowels:

fetching *fudge* *sticker* *fuzzy*

Spelling and reading patterns are based on one or both of these principles. Lesson plans will very explicitly take students through the steps so they can understand *why* words are spelled a certain way, based upon these principles. (Bishop, 1985)

Learning how to break the English code can be exciting detective work. The exploration of language of origin of a word, as well as the orthographic/spelling patterns or regularities identified by Hanna, et al. (1996) provide two strong conceptual bases for spelling and reading, as well as determining the meaning and function of words.

Approaching spelling and reading from the perspective of investigating recurrent patterns, rather than memorizing every word, makes the act of spelling and reading a manageable feat rather than an insurmountable task.

This approach is designed to make spelling and reading individual words a conscious act in which students can think their way through the questions, "How do I spell this word?"

and "How do I read this word?" rather than having to memorize every word. *"Students need strategies to digest information about English spelling patterns without frustration".* (Kearns & Whaley, 2019)

Developmental Issues and Grade Level Norms

It is important when teaching kindergarten students to begin by teaching the Anglo-Saxon skills: the single consonants, consonant digraphs, and the single vowels (Lessons 1-4). Spend a week or more on each of these lessons, depending upon how efficiently and accurately your students assimilate the ideas and skills.

When teaching first graders, teach everything that was taught to the kindergarten students, perhaps moving through Lessons 1-4 more quickly. The lessons in Section III teach spelling patterns that are based on the Position Principle: vowel digraphs, Vowel plus E, "au-aw", vowel diphthongs, "ou-ow", "oi-oy", R-controlled vowels, and Two Vowel Friends.

Teach first and second grade students the more *sophisticated* consonant sound/letter correspondences: "c," "g," "y," "x", and "qu". The sophistication of these consonants is based upon the fact that these letters can represent more than one sound: "c" says /k/ and /s/, "g" says /g/ and /j/, "y" says /i/, /ee/, /ie/, and "qu" says /kw/. All of these consonant lessons can also be explained by the Position Principle.

A second group of orthographic patterns are explained and organized based on the Protection Principle in Section III, and these too can be taught in late first and second grades. The weak and strong vowel lesson is the first lesson in this group because all of the rules in this category are based upon the idea of weak vowels needing extra consonants to protect their sound, and strong vowels not being in need of extra consonants for protection. The order of lessons in this category are: FLoSS, k/ck, ch/tch, ge/dge, most kind old pink things.

In Section IV, syllable concepts and types are taught, as well as the past tense concepts, doubling the last consonant when adding suffixes, plurals, drop the "e", and change "y" to "i" when suffixes are added to words. Because first and second grade texts and books have two-syllable words, students in these grades need to learn syllable types.

If older students in third grade and above have not yet been introduced to the linguistic concepts taught in Lessons 1-4 and the one-syllable orthographic patterns, they need to be introduced to these ideas. The pace of teaching will depend upon the students' mastery of the ideas, as well as how efficient their phonological and phonemic awareness skills are.

For older students, the sequence of teaching syllable types can be intertwined with the orthographic patterns and the lessons that teach the various vowel identities. After you teach the single vowels and single consonants, a logical subsequent lesson would be to teach closed syllables and then open syllables. After you teach the Vowel plus E lesson, teach the Vowel plus E syllable. After teaching the R-controlled vowel lesson, teach the R-controlled syllable. After teaching the vowel digraphs and diphthongs, teach the vowel team syllable. Finally, teach the consonant LE syllable.

First and second graders are expected to read simple, then complex one-syllable words followed by two-syllable words. In first and second grade, students need to learn the inflectional suffixes, past tense, plurals, "-ing" and "-ly," as well as Anglo-Saxon prefixes and compound words. In second and third grade, students are expected to learn Latin prefixes, suffixes, and roots. In fourth grade and above, students begin to learn the Greek layer of English.

Individual Learning Pace and Skills

Although each student will have to proceed through the same sequence of skills, they will come to the act of learning with different levels of processing. Lesson plans and teaching schedules must consider each student's phonemic awareness skills, working and long-term memory skills, and general learning abilities. Also, the age of the student, as well as whether they are in beginning or intermediate elementary grades, middle school, high school, or college, or are adult learners, will affect lesson plan execution. Further, considering what skills students have been taught, and which they have mastered, influences the student's rate of acquisition of new material.

Assessment: Letters and Their Sounds, Spelling and Reading of Words

For all students, regardless of their age, assessment of what they know, what they are confused about, and what they have or have not been taught is the initial step in determining learning goals. Ascertaining which consonants and vowels they know in isolation, which letters they are confused about, and what they do not know will determine the starting goals for teaching them to read and spell accurately. A spelling and reading test will illustrate which orthographic patterns and syllable types they know, and because phonological processing is also a key set of skills, administration of a phonological processing and phonemic awareness test is suggested.

These three points in time are crucial for assessing a student's skills:

- When work begins with an individual student or with a group of students, determining what they have mastered is essential. Discovering what they have partially mastered in past learning experiences, and/or what misinformation they have construed, must be addressed. Also, determining what skills or concepts they have never been exposed to, or those which they have forgotten, will guide instructional goals.

- Once concepts have been introduced, doing activities that allow the students to use what they have learned will shed light on how much practice is needed with this new information. What are they confusing? Has this idea not registered at all?

- Finally, retention of information over time must be assessed. What did a student retain from yesterday's lesson, at the beginning of the week or from last week? Are the ideas that were worked on last month still an active part of a students' reading/spelling repertoire?

Ways to Glean Information

Writing the Alphabet

When you initially ask students to write the alphabet, it will be instructional to see if they ask whether they should write the lower- or upper-case alphabet and in the printed or cursive styles. Ask them to first write the lower-case alphabet, and leave the option open whether they are to print or write in cursive, because asking why they prefer printing to cursive again gives insight into their skills. Also important is checking to see if they know the names of each letter. Observe them closely as they write the alphabet, looking for:

- How they hold their writing instrument.
- How close to the paper they work. If the student works within four to six inches of the paper they may be having visual acuity problems.
- If they can print the entire alphabet without having to say the sequence aloud multiple times, which may indicate sequential memory issues.
- If they have omitted any letters.
- How the student forms the letters, whether they begin and end in the proper place, and if they have portrayed the relative size of the letters accurately.

All of this information can lead to setting a goal for handwriting, as well as a goal for learning the names of the letters.

The program *Handwriting Without Tears* masterfully teaches the shapes of letters, the spatial qualities of the letters, and an internal dialogue which helps the learner know how to form each letter.

Determining Knowledge of Letter/Sound Relationships

Next assess which consonant and vowel letter/sound relations the student knows in isolation. Give them a list the consonants and vowels, then ask them to state all of the sounds that they know for each of the letters, because some letters have more than one sound (like "c," "g," "y," "x" and many vowels).

Appendix B contains samples of a student sheet and a page on which to record students' answers. The results of this exercise will establish the sound/symbol correspondence goals required for each student. Copying the student sheet onto bright paper and placing it in a plastic sleeve makes it easy to use for many students.

Obtaining Levels of Reading and Spelling Proficiency

Use standardized or norm referenced reading and spelling tests to identify the words and reading/spelling patterns your students know. There are two commercial tests which include a variety of words that represent the common orthographic patterns in English, *The Test of Written Spelling* and *Words Their Way*. These tests assess many spelling patterns on multiple grade levels and include high frequency words and phonetically regular words.

The *Slosson Test*, the *Woodcock Johnson Test*, and the *Wechsler Achievement Test* all have excellent word recognition tests that can be analyzed to provide teachers with diagnostic feedback for setting teaching goals.

Analyzing Mistakes

Students' mistakes are valuable. When a student makes a mistake, their thinking process is more evident than if they immediately answer correctly. If students spell or read a word accurately, you can ask them to explain why they did so *after* acknowledging that they were indeed correct.

If a student makes a mistake in spelling or reading, ask yourself:

- What is correct about this answer?
- What is the student confusing?
- What is incorrect, and what type of a mistake is it?

There are several *types* of mistakes a student can make when she is spelling or reading an individual word:

- Does the student represent the correct number and order of sounds?
- If she spells *spend* as *send*, she may not have heard the word correctly, or she may not be holding onto the entire sequence of sounds, a phonological memory mistake. Ask her to repeat the word in order to ascertain whether she heard the word correctly, and/or whether she is pronouncing the word accurately, because if you don't hear or say a word accurately, you can't spell it accurately.
- If she spells or reads the word *jumps* as *jumsp*, she has probably made a sequencing error.
- Has she left out a sound within the word, spelling or reading *split* as *spit*?
- Has she added a sound to the word *clasp* by writing *claspt*?
- Has she substituted a voiced sound for an unvoiced sound, reading *patted* as *padded*? Has she substituted one vowel sound for another similar sounding vowel, spelling *spill* as *spell*, or *pauper* as *popper*? These are phonemic awareness errors.
- Does she not know the letter that represents a sound? If she can pronounce the word *send*, after also accurately reading it, but spells it *sind*, this is a letter/sound error.
- Does she not know a particular spelling rule or pattern? This may be indicated if her spelling of *shake* is *shak* or *shack*; *know* is *now*; or *knife* is *nife*.
- Does she confuse the spelling rules? If her spelling of *rake* is *raik*, or *break* is *braek*, this may be the case.

It doesn't matter what list of words you use for your test, if you analyze the errors a student consistently makes, you will be able to design your teaching based upon their performance.

What Errors Can Indicate

If your student is adding sounds, leaving out sounds, substituting sounds or shifting the order of the sounds, they are probably having phonemic awareness problems. In this case, adding one of a number of excellent tests for phonological processing problems to your testing procedures like the *Comprehensive Test of Phonological Processing* (CTOPP-2) is recommended. Phonemic awareness activities are also included in lessons presented in this book.

If your student is substituting voiced and unvoiced consonants or similar vowel sounds, that student needs to be taught those concepts explicitly. See *How to Teach the Consonants* or *How to Teach the Vowels* in Lessons 1-4 of Part II in this book.

If your student is making orthographic mistakes, you will know which lessons to emphasize in your lesson plans from Part III.

Structure of the Lessons in This Book

The lessons in this book are built on teacher/student dialogues that actively engage the students, with the format for each lesson following a specific pattern.

/a/ /t/ **Reading/Spelling Patterns** are named, and the number of words in Hanna, et al. (1996) are given for that pattern. This number can be used to show the student how valuable the spelling/reading pattern will be for them because it helps them to thoughtfully spell a specific number of words. Each lesson focuses on only one spelling pattern.

 Concepts in each lesson are designed to provide teachers with the specific, relevant ideas that underlie the skills taught in the lesson.

Introductions will describe the ideas that will be taught to the students. At the beginning of each lesson, ask students what they already know about the spelling pattern you are teaching by querying, "What do you already know about this spelling pattern?" Frequently students will surprise you with how much they truly do know, therefore this practice enhances their feelings of mastery and academic self-esteem. At other times, their answers will allow you to see and hear what they are confused about, or even erroneous in, regarding their understanding of the concept. This information tells the teacher how to modify a lesson, as well as how to correct misconceptions that students hold.

The ideas presented in each introduction are a possible, but not exclusive, way of speaking to your students about the learning goal of each lesson. Tailoring the ideas to the vocabulary of individual students is the best approach.

Lists of Words demonstrate a lesson's focus, as well as words which are non-examples of the concept of the lesson, and are provided so students can actively learn new skill sets and the concepts they are built upon. You can add words to the lists that are appropriate to your student's oral vocabulary by writing them on the board or an overhead, or by creating sets of words written on card stock which students can sort in a pocket chart. Students can also create their own sets of words for sorting by using stickies or cards, but be sure to use only six to ten words in any given lesson.

Read the words aloud to your students or ask them if they want to volunteer to read one or two words to ensure humiliation protection.

 The Teacher/Student Dialogue is the heart of each lesson. This section provides you as the teacher with a specific set of ideas and questions to ask the students to aid them in discovering the linguistic ideas, orthographic patterns, and syllable types. Questions for asking students are in bold print, and the answers are italicized. Exceptions to the rules are not presented during the initial lessons because we want the students to have the experience of English being logical and predicable.

Here are some samples questions that you will use in the lessons:

- How many sounds are in each of these words?
- What letters map onto or represent those sounds?
- How are the sounds in these words the same?
- How are the letters in these words different?
- Where does this particular orthographic pattern occur in the words: the beginning, the middle, or the end of the word or syllable?
- How can we account for the differences: the Position Principle, the Protection Principle, or both?

Teachers are encouraged to ask questions with possible alternate answers to frame the students' thinking:

- "How many sounds are in this word, *three or four*?"
- "Does the c sound like */k/ or /s/* in this word?"
- "What letter comes after the c, *a vowel or a consonant*?"
- "Is the vowel in this word *weak or strong, protected or unprotected*?"

By using these types of questions, you are teaching the learner to question herself intelligently while helping her to access and compare the relevant information rather than guessing wildly. In addition, you enhance her academic self-esteem because she will be highly accurate when questioned in this way.

After training students to think in this manner, you will eventually be able to scaffold the process by asking questions without alternatives. When a student says, "You don't have to ask me questions, just give me time to think of them myself," you have entered teacher heaven!

Employ as many sensory and cognitive representations of the information as possible by:

- Using boxes to represent the number of sounds in a word.
- Using different colors to distinguish between types of letters, consonants, vowels, or specific spelling/reading patterns that map onto sounds.

- Writing down the student's ideas on the board and in a rule book.

- Using diagrams or cards of the thinking steps that you have created together.

- Using a tool bar to jog the student's memory of the spelling patterns.

 Practice is always essential, with different learners in need of varying numbers of exposures to concepts in order to assimilate enough information to begin using that information as part of their spelling and reading repertoire. In addition, because the human brain prefers novelty over repetition, practice must also be varied. Games and computer programs can help when practicing new concepts, while questions posed about the concepts will stabilize the new ideas much more readily than repetitive, thoughtless paper and pencil tasks. Having student construct their own games, and teaching others what they have learned, can all contribute to a more interesting and engaging learning environment.

Review is another key component, as no one can be presented with a new concept only once and hope to generalize it to the rest of their lives and learning. Because each person is quite unique, some students will need more exposures to an idea than others. Review, like practice, can become drudgery—or it can be thoughtful and creative.

Here are a few concepts that will be useful when designing review activities:

- **Chunk size** refers to the number of ideas included in review activities (two, three, or four rules). Once students have demonstrated mastery, with eighty percent accuracy or greater over several activities, having them work on an assignment that involves two orthographic patterns will build their flexibility of thinking. You can eventually have them work with three or four patterns simultaneously, with a true test of their knowledge of those patterns being when they can read or spell a random list of words and name the spelling pattern(s) that governs each one.

- **Frequency** refers to how often a particular child needs to experience concepts in order to stabilize them, with learners varying significantly in this regard.

- **Variety** refers to the format used when practicing spelling lists. Crossword puzzles, a variety of games, computer games, creating stories, and dictating sentences can all be utilized during review. Writing out step cards with students, or having them define spelling patterns in their own words, can assist with this process, while displaying these memory helpers around the classroom helps students refer back to the information when working on assignments. Be sure to mix and match these activities to align your lessons with your students' interests and attention spans.

Technical Literacy Vocabulary

Each and every academic discipline has its own vocabulary and specific concepts that allow educators to be precise, accurate, and readily understood.

Mathematicians talk about numerators, denominators, factors and rational numbers, minuend and subtrahend. Language Arts teachers work with expository and narrative texts, exploring plot, setting, and characters. Geographers speak about continental drift, oceans, glaciers, and plains. Literacy too has its own technical vocabulary, and the curriculum of reading and spelling also has a lexicon.

Finding a common language can indeed be a challenge. On the one hand, you don't want the terms you use to teach literacy to be so basic that remedial students once again feel that they are being talked down to. Conversely, using technical language can be confusing and pedantic, causing both teachers and students at all grade levels to ask in exasperation, "Why can't you just say that in simple words?"

Thus, in order to address both sides of this issue, common terms, as well as technical terms, are used throughout this book. That said, educators must remember to consistently display a respectful tone and attitude for their students, which will bridge the first forays into using the lexicon of literacy. The best approach is to first define, then use technical terms with your students, while being sure to observe how they react.

For easy reference, a list of linguistic terms is located in the Glossary at the end of this book.

Planning Lessons

You can refer to the following list when planning lessons:

1. Frequently examine the literacy testing and goals set for each student in order to determine if your lessons are reflecting the student's learning needs.

2. Decide whether skills worked on in the last week, the past month, or even in the last couple of months should be reviewed. Consistent record keeping makes it easy to know which skills have been taught, as well as when to revisit those lessons.

3. Using the information gathered in Step 1 and Step 2, ask yourself:
   - "How can I use a variety of activities?
   - What activities do I want to use to reinforce the new skill I am teaching?
   - Can I do a word sort, use a game or give a writing assignment?
   - What resources do I have in my library of curriculum tools that can be used to teach this lesson?
   - Do I want my students to read and/or spell individual words, phrases, or sentences or read connected or decodable texts?
   - How can I actively engage students with something other than just a worksheet?

4. Consider which new skills are going to be directly taught in each lesson. The sequence of lessons in this book, along with your record keeping document will help to determine what has already been taught, as well as what to teach next in a logical sequence.

5. Look up which lesson in this book teaches the new skills that you are targeting in each lesson plan to remind you which questions to ask, what words to use, and the principles of spelling to include for directly teaching a new skill.

6. Write out a list of words for your students to read and spell that exemplifies the skill being taught in each lesson.

7. Plan a phonemic awareness activity with the skills you are working on.

8. Pick a fluency activity for students to do.

9. Find or adapt a game that uses the skills being taught in the lesson.

10. Decide upon what home practice activities your students should do.

Part II

Sound/Letter Correspondences

Sound/Letter Correspondences

How to Teach the Consonants

Teaching the consonants in an explicit manner should be done for several reasons. When initially teaching sound/symbol correspondence to any learner, it is quite useful for them to see and *experience* patterns and categories of ideas that are reliable and functional. Because human brains like to organize ideas and file them logically in memory, presenting the consonants in this manner aids in the learner's ability to store and retrieve information about these abstract squiggles called *letters*.

Another important reason for teaching the consonants with an emphasis on articulation is that students will learn to pronounce the sounds correctly. While certainly useful even for general education students, this is extremely beneficial for students with dyslexia, learning disabilities, phonemic awareness problems or those who are English Language Learners. Many students with reading challenges have been *taught* the sound/letter relationships, but have not actually *learned* them, which is why teaching the articulatory features is a more coherent way of illustrating the facts and concepts about consonants. This active, constructive procedure demands that students think through the learning experience and by making the information more meaningful, students will remember the sound/letter pairings more accurately.

Consonants are identified as *closed* sounds, and are grouped based upon the fact that a common part of the mouth, lips, tongue, teeth, or throat holds back the air when they are articulated. The quality of the airflow is also used when categorizing the consonants.

Every consonant is either *voiced* or *unvoiced*. Voiced means that the vocal cords are vibrating as a phoneme is sounded, unvoiced means that the vocal cords are not vibrating.

Put your fingers gently on your voice box, then say /s/ and /z/ to feel the difference between unvoiced and voiced consonants. Another way to test for the voiced and unvoiced quality of consonants is to put your hands over your ears. You will clearly hear the difference between voiced and unvoiced consonants or vowels.

If a student is uncertain about whether a consonant is voiced or unvoiced, you can ask them to gently touch your voice box in order to feel the difference. Ask a question with two possible answers to focus the student on how a particular letter is articulated: "Is /p/ unvoiced like /s/ or voiced like /z/?"

These factors group the consonants into pairs or groups because each letter in the pair or group is articulated in a similar manner. If you use your tongue behind the top teeth for one consonant in a pair, you will do the same for the partner. One of the consonants in a pair will be voiced and one always unvoiced, while the air quality will be the same for both letters in the pair.

Three critical elements need to be included when teaching the consonants, which can be accomplished by asking students:

- What part of the mouth is primarily working when you make this sound?
- What is the quality of the air produced by this consonant?
- Is this consonant voiced or unvoiced?

Each of the attributes of the consonants will thus become a part of a teaching/learning interchange that gives the learner another input system for accurate pronunciation of the sound, while serving to stabilize a paired association with the letter (Moats, 2014).

Many of the most common spelling errors are substitutions of the letters that form these voiced or unvoiced consonant pairs. Students often misspell *tardy* as *tarty*, substituting a "t" for a "d". Other mistakes can happen among consonants with the same air quality. Many students frequently substitute the fricatives "f" for "th," or "s" for "sh," because the sound attributes of these letters are so similar. Once a student knows the articulation features of each letter, it becomes easier to talk with them about these mistakes.

The teaching dialogues in the lessons for the consonant pairs or groups have specific questions and appropriate answers for each consonant group.

The following *linguistic labels* for the different classes of consonants are based upon their articulation features, and it will be up to the teacher whether or not to use these labels to name the consonant groups when working with students.

- **Stops** are formed by closing or blocking air flow, and then exploding a puff of air: /p/, /b/, /t/, /d/, /k/, /g/.
- **Fricatives** are formed by narrowing the air channel and then forcing the air through it, creating friction in the mouth: /f/, /v/, /th/, /s/, /z/, /sh/, /zh/.
- **Affricatives** are the sounds produced by the sequence of a stop followed by a fricative: /ch/, /j/.
- **Nasals** are formed when the mouth is closed off by the lips or tongue, forcing the air through the nose: /m/, /n/, /ng/.
- **Laterals** are formed by interrupting the airflow slightly, with no resulting friction as the air comes out the sides of the tongue: /l/, /r/.
- **Semivowels** are formed in similar ways to the vowels with an open mouth and a continual air stream: /wh/, /w/, /h/, /y/.

The different categories of consonants include:

- Single consonants are one letter mapping onto one sound: "b," "d," "f," "l".
- Consonant digraphs have two letters mapping onto one sound: "ch," "sh," "wh".
- Consonant blends contain two letters and two sounds at the beginning of a word or syllable like "bl-" and "pr-," or at the end of a word or syllable like "-ct" and "-mp".
- Consonant clusters contain three letters mapping onto three sounds: "str-," "scr-".

It is valuable for students to be able to identify and categorize consonants into these groups in order to organize the information concisely and efficiently in their minds.

One way to represent the concepts of how the consonants are organized is to create Two-Column Notes.

Consonants

Single Consonants	One letter, one sound: "p," "b," "t," "d," "k," "s"
Consonant Digraphs	Two letters, one sound: "sh," "ch," "wh," "-ng"
Consonant Blends	Two letters, two sounds, which can be in the beginning or end of a word with initial or final blends: "sl-," "pr-," "cl-" = initial blends "-ct," "-nd," "-pt" = final blends
Consonant Clusters	Three letters, three sounds which can only be in the beginning of a word or syllable: "str-," "scr-"

How to Teach the Vowels

When teaching vowels, the second group of letters in the English language, it is helpful to present an alternative way to learn the sounds they make. Rather than only saying each vowel out loud, and relying on the students' auditory input system, the articulation system should be explored and defined.

Vowels are created in the mouth by the interaction of the lips, tongue, and jaw, and it is useful to illustrate how each part of the mouth is working:

- The lips can be pulled back in a smile, open and relaxed or puckered forward and closed.
- The jaw can be open or closed.
- The tongue can be in a high position in the front of the mouth, a low and flat position in the middle of the mouth, or high in the back of the mouth.

All vowels are voiced, and the sound differences between them are minute, so it is important to provide students with the above information about how they form the sounds in their mouth.

Categories of vowels include:

- Single vowels, single letters with a single sound.
- Vowel digraphs, two letters with a single sound.
- Vowel diphthongs, two letters that are formed in the mouth by gliding from one jaw, lip, or tongue position to another.

Vowels have some unique jobs in spelling:

- Every word in the English language must have at least one vowel sound.
- The vowels contained in a word are often a clue to the spelling rules being applied in them.
- The vowels in each word are the key to "sounding them out". By finding the vowel, and remembering the sound that goes along with each letter, you can say and hold onto the sound, then spell or read the word easily.

Vowels have greater variations in pronunciation and spelling patterns than consonants. A single vowel like "a" can say its letter name in an open syllable, as in *apron*. The same single vowel can say its "short" sound in a closed syllable, as in the word *can*, or /u/, the schwa sound, in an unaccented syllable as in the word *aboard*.

Teaching our students each of these possibilities slowly over time, while also emphasizing the need for flexibility of thinking will help them become efficient, thoughtful spellers and readers.

Using two-column notes, we can summarize the following information about vowels which is presented in many of the lessons about vowels.

Vowels

Single Vowels	One letter, one sound: a, e, i, o, u
Vowel Digraphs	Two letters, one sound: oo, au, aw Vowel plus E vowels: a-e, ee, i-e, o-e, u-e R-controlled vowels: ir, ur, er, ar, or Two vowel friends: ea-ey-y, ai-ay, oa-ow
Vowel Diphthongs	Two letters formed when the mouth glides from one position to another: oi-oy, ou-ow

After this lengthy introduction for teachers, we now turn to a lesson that will help you teach these concepts to your students, one step at a time.

Each lesson has many activities. Depending on the size of your class, you may choose to present the first concepts to the whole class. You can also divide and conquer by teaching your students some concepts in a whole group setting, then reinforcing the concepts with activities in smaller groups. Be sure to note which students are learning activities quickly, because they can then become peer tutors, working with students who need more time and practice.

Lessons are designed to span several days, or even weeks, depending on the pace of your students' learning, with each lesson providing background information and concepts as well as a possible introduction. Questions to ask the students, along with possible answers in italics, follow these brief introductions. Phonemic awareness activities and games will accompany each lesson.

_____

_____

_____

_____

_____

_____

_____

_____

_____

_____

_____

_____

_____

_____

_____

_____

_____

_____

LESSON 1

Sound/Symbol Correspondences:

"p," "b," "t," "d," "k," "g," "i," "a," "o," "e," "u"

Concepts

 The consonants that are to be presented in this lesson are single consonants, while the vowels are single vowels. In addition, the articulation features of each sound/letter consonant duo will be explored. You can make this lesson as simple or as complex as you need to by including or excluding linguistic terms. For further concepts and ideas for introducing this lesson, please refer to *How to Teach the Consonants* and *How to Teach the Vowels*.

If this lesson is the initial teaching of these concepts to younger students, practice the sound/symbol associations by having the students read and spell individual words and phrases, as well as by playing games with them. Phonemic awareness activities are also included as a supportive and **necessary** activity.

For older students, this will be a brief but informative lesson, and a great deal of practice will not be needed. However, the concepts of consonant pairs, the articulation features of each of the letters/sounds, and the labels of single consonants and single vowels are integral to the lessons that follow.

The Teacher – Student Learning Dialogue scripts can be used to teach the concepts in each sample lesson. Questions and ideas for teachers to share appear in **bold** type, with possible answers shown in ***bold italicized type.***

During this lesson, we are going to see how our language is built by investigating single letters that combine to create words to read or spell.

Either a consonant or a vowel letter can represent a single sound or phoneme. Consonants are known as closed phonemes because some part of our mouth—lips, tongue, or teeth—closes off the air.

In the English alphabet, the letters "a," "e," "i," "o," "u" are vowels. The other letters are consonants. The letter "y" can be categorized as both a consonant and a vowel, depending on its position in a word.

Vowels are known as open phonemes because we open our mouth in a fixed position and exhale air to produce their sound. All of the vowels are shaped in our mouth using the tongue, jaw, and lips. All vowels are voiced and vowels have unique jobs in spelling.

Every word in the English language must have at least one vowel sound, and because the vowels contained in words are often a clue to the spelling rule, they are the key to "sounding out" any word—if you can find the vowel and remember the sound that goes along with the letter(s), you can say and hold onto the sound, then spell or read the word easily.

Consonants are sorted into pairs or groups. In this lesson we will focus on three pairs or consonant partners.

Each consonant in a pair uses the same part of the mouth to block off the air, while one member of the pair is voiced, and the other is unvoiced.

Voiced means that the vocal cords are vibrating as a sound is made. Unvoiced means that the vocal cords are not vibrating. Put your hand gently on your voice box and say /s/, then say /z/—which letter is vibrating or voiced? Which letter is not vibrating or unvoiced (/s/ = unvoiced; /z/ = voiced)

The consonants in this lesson are single consonants, which are a single letter that stands for a single sound. The vowels in this lesson are single vowels, and are a single letter that stands for a single sound.

• • • •

Remember, you don't need to present all of these ideas on the first day of this lesson. Choose one or two ideas under the consonant and vowel sections, then build up the ideas over several days.

Before teaching new ideas, always ascertain what your students know and/or confuse about the current concept by asking them: *"What do you remember about these letters?"*

_____
_____
_____
_____
_____
_____
_____
_____
_____
_____
_____
_____
_____

The Single Consonants

Teacher – Student Learning Dialogue

Introduction

In the alphabet, we have two types of letters. Do you know the two types of letters in the alphabet? *Consonants and vowels*

If students do not know this answer, the teacher will say:

Consonants and vowels are the two types of letters used in the alphabet. We will look at those now:

> The letter "a" is a vowel.
> The letter "b" is a consonant.

The teacher now goes through the alphabet, asking the students to sort the letters into groups of consonants and vowels, and labeling each letter as a single consonant or a single vowel.

Consonants are called closed phonemes because we close off the air with our lips or tongue. Each consonant also has a particular type of air, a stream or a puff. Each consonant either makes our voice box vibrate, which we call a voiced consonant, or our voice box does not vibrate, which we call an unvoiced consonant.

The consonants that we are going to learn today, which come in pairs, are two different letters that are formed by using the same part of your mouth and the same air—however, one of the consonants in a pair will be unvoiced, and one will be voiced.

Teaching the Letter "p"

First, I am going to say a sound and ask you to repeat it, then I will ask you some questions about how you pronounced that sound.

The name of this letter is "p," which sounds like /p/. Please say this sound.

- When you say this sound, what part of your mouth are you using to form the sound, your lips or your tongue? *Lips*
- Is the air coming out of your lips in a stream like /s/ or a puff /t/? *Puff*
- Is this sound voiced or unvoiced? *Unvoiced*

Finding the Partner of "p" by Comparing it to "t," "k," "b"

Let's find the voiced partner of P. The partners use the same part of the mouth, the same action and they create the same type of air. One letter in the pair will be unvoiced, in this case, P, and the other partner will be voiced.

Please say the sounds, /p,t/.

- Did you use your lips when you said /t/ like when you said /p/? *No*
- Is the air coming out of your mouth in a puff like /p/ when you say /t/? *Yes*
- Is /t/ voiced? *No*

Because the answer is "no" to these two of these questions, T is not the partner of P.

Please say the sounds, /p,k/.

- Did you use your lips when you said /k/ like when you said /p/? *No*
- Is the air coming out of your mouth in a puff like /p/ when you say /k/? *Yes*
- Is /k/ voiced? *No*

Because the answer is "no" to these two of these questions, K is not the partner of P.

Please say the sounds, /p,b/.

- Did you use your lips when you said /b/ like when you said /p/? Yes
- Is the air coming out of your mouth in a puff like /p/ when you say /b/? Yes
- Is /b/ voiced? Yes

Because the answer is "yes" to these three questions, B is the partner of P.

Teaching the Letter "t"

The name of this letter is "t". It sounds like /t/, please say this sound.

- When you say this sound, what part of your mouth are you using to form the sound, your lips or your tongue? *Tongue*
- Are you using the front of your tongue behind your teeth, or the back of your tongue? *Front of the tongue*
- Is your tongue sticking out, or does it touch behind your upper front teeth? *Behind my upper front teeth*
- Is the air coming out of your mouth in a stream, or in a puff? *Puff*
- Is this sound/letter voiced, or unvoiced? *Unvoiced*

Finding the Partner of "t" by Comparing it to "f," "d," "g"

Let's find the voiced partner of "t".

Partners use the same part of the mouth, do the same action, and create the same type of air. One letter in the pair will be unvoiced, in this case "t," and the other partner will be voiced.

Please say the sounds /t and f/.

- When you say /f/, did you use your tongue behind your front upper teeth like /t/? *No*
- Is the air coming out in a puff like /t/? *No*
- Is /f/ voiced? *No*

Because the answer is "no" to three of these questions, "f" is not the partner of "t".

Please say the sounds /t/ and /g/.

- When you say /g/, did you use your tongue behind your front teeth like /t/? *No*
- Is the air coming out in a puff like /t/? *Yes*
- Is /g/ voiced? *Yes*

Because the answer is "no" to one of these questions, "k" is not the partner of "t".

Please say the sounds /t/ and /d/.

- When you say /d/, did you use your tongue behind your front teeth like /t/? *Yes*
- Is the air coming out in a puff like /t/? *Yes*
- Is /d/ voiced? *Yes*

Because the answer is "yes" to all of these questions, "d" is the partner of "t".

Teaching the Letter "k"

The name of this letter is "k," it says /k/, please repeat this sound.

- When you say this sound, what part of your mouth are you using to form the sound, your lips or your tongue? *Tongue*
- Are you using the front of your tongue behind your teeth or the back of your tongue? *Back of the tongue*
- Is your tongue resting on the bottom of your mouth when you say /k/ or does it touch the roof of your mouth in the back? *It briefly touches the roof of the mouth*
- Is the air coming out of your mouth in a stream or a puff? *Puff*
- Is this sound voiced or unvoiced? *Unvoiced*

Finding the Partner of "k" by Comparing it to "s," "j," "g"

Let's find the voiced partner of "k". The partners use the same part of the mouth, do the same actions, and create the same type of air. One letter in the pair will be unvoiced, in this case "k," and the other partner will be voiced.

Please say the sounds /k/ and /s/.

- Are you using the back of your tongue like /k/ when you say /s/? *No*
- Is the air coming out of your mouth in a puff like /k/? *No*
- Is /s/ voiced? *No*

Because the answer is "no" to three of these questions, "k" is not the partner of "s".

Please say the sounds /k/ and /j/.

- When you say /j/, do you use your back of your tongue like/k/? *No*
- Is the air coming out of your mouth in a puff like /k/? *Yes*
- Is /j/ voiced? *Yes*

Because the answer is "no" to one of these questions, "k" is not the partner of "j".

Please say the sounds /k/ and /g/.

- When you say /g/, do you use your back tongue like /k/? *Yes*
- Is the air coming out of your mouth in a puff like /k/? *Yes*
- Is /g/ voiced? *Yes*

The letters "k" and "g" are a consonant pair, or consonant partners. You use the same part of your mouth to make the sounds and the air is the same, but they are different letters, and "k" is unvoiced while "g" is voiced.

The Single Vowel Staircase

Teacher – Student Learning Dialogue

Introduction

Vowels are defined as open phonemes because we position our lips, tongue, and jaw in various stable positions while pronouncing the vowel sound. All vowels are voiced phonemes.

There are two categories of vowels:

- Single vowels have one letter, one sound.
- Vowel teams, vowel digraphs and diphthongs, have two or more vowel letters that make one vowel sound.

In this lesson, we will be learning about single vowels. Because it is challenging to see the inside of our mouth as we create the vowel sounds, we are going to use a picture called the Single Vowel Staircase to show how our jaw, lips, and tongue are positioned when we say the single vowels out loud.

When we say the single vowel sounds, our lips and jaw are in different positions:

- The lips, which are shaped like a smile at the top of the staircase, will gradually open as we move down the staircase.
- At the top of the staircase, the jaw is closed, and with every step down, it opens a little bit, until it is quite open at the bottom of the staircase.

Show your students this **Single Vowel Staircase** image as you explain these ideas.

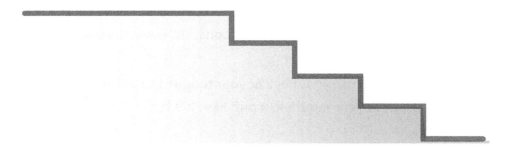

Be sure to compare all of the vowel letters and vowel sounds *before* putting them on the staircase. Place them in order on the board or a desk, and once in order, place them on the staircase.

We want to pay particular attention to how open or closed our jaw feels. Here's a way to tell how open or closed your jaw is.

CLOSED JAW

OPEN JAW

Please put your fingers on your cheek, and your thumb below your jaw, so you can feel the movement, then say /i/ and /a/.

- Did your jaw open or close when you said these sounds? You will use your hand on your cheek to judge how open or closed two sounds are. *Open*

Teaching the Single Vowels

Please repeat the sounds of these two single vowels, /i/ and/o/.

- Which one is your jaw more closed on when you say these sounds? */i/ is more closed*

- On which is your jaw more open? */o/ is open*

The letter "i" goes higher on the staircase, and "o" goes lower.

This is how we use the idea of the staircase to represent the jaw positions:

i

o

Let's compare these two sounds /i/ and /a/.

- Which one is your jaw more closed on when you say these sounds? */i/ is more closed*
- On which is your jaw more open? */a/ is open*

The "i" will go higher on the staircase, and the "a" will go lower.

Now let's compare /a/ and /o/.

- Which one is your jaw more closed on when you say these sounds? */a/ is more closed*
- On which one is your jaw more open? */o/ is open*

The letter "a" sits between the "i" and the "o" on the staircase.

i

a

o

Let's compare /i/ and /u/.

- Which one is your jaw more closed on when you say these sounds? */i/ is more closed*
- On which is your jaw more open? */u/ is open*

The letter "u" goes lower on the staircase than "i".

Now let's compare /u/ and /o/.

- Which one is your jaw more closed on when you say these sounds? */u/ is more closed*
- On which is your jaw more open? */o/ is more open*

The letter "u" goes higher on the staircase than "o".

Now let's compare /u/ and /a/.

- Which one is your mouth more closed on when you say these sounds? */a/.*
- Which one is your mouth open when you say these sounds? */u/*

The letter "u" sits between "a" and "o".

i

a

u

o

Let's compare "e" to all of the other single vowels.

- With the sounds of /e/ and /o/, which is your jaw more closed on? /e/
- On which is your jaw more open? */o/ is open*

The "e" sits higher on the staircase than "o".

Now let's compare /e/ and /u/.

- Which one is your jaw more closed on when you say these sounds? /e/
- On which is your jaw more open? */u/ is open.*

The "e" sits higher on the staircase than the "u".

Now let's compare /e/ and /a/.

- Which one is your jaw more closed on when you say these sounds? */e/ is more closed*
- Which one is your jaw more open? */a/ is open.*

The "e" sits higher on the staircase than the "a".

Now let's compare /e/ and /i/.

- **Which one is your jaw more closed on when you say these sounds?** */i/ is more closed*
- **On which one is your jaw more open?** */e/ is open*

The "e" sits lower on the staircase than the "i".

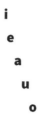

We need to check ourselves. Please put your hand on your cheek and say these sounds in order to see if your jaw starts out closed and opens in little baby steps to the most open position: /i/, /e/, /a/, /u/, /o/

Here is the Single Vowel Staircase with the letters in order from the most closed jaw position to the most open. The lips will start in a smile, and then slowly open in a relaxed position.

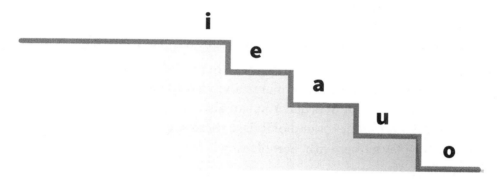

We will practice all the consonant and vowel sounds we have learned in this lesson by reading and spelling words, doing phonemic awareness activities, and playing games with them.

Hints for Teaching and Practicing the Consonants and Vowels Actively

1. Have an enlarged picture of the head and mouth on the board or overhead so you can point to the parts of the mouth as you ask questions and/or discuss the consonants and vowels.

2. Have students look at their mouths in a mirror to help them in answering your questions.

3. Use pictures of the mouth to reinforce each consonant pair or vowel sound. A great resource for these pictures is the *Dialogue Cards for How to Teach Reading and Spelling, Bringing the Science into the Classroom.*

4. Be sure to have the students feel the voiced and unvoiced quality of the consonants and vowels, not just listen for it.

5. Be sure to say the pure sound of each consonant. Don't add the sound /u/ to each consonant: /t/ is *not* /tu/.

6. Once you have taught these letters and their sounds, you can practice them by showing the letter and asking your students to give you the sound or you can say the sound and have them hold up a card with the letter printed on it.

7. You can ask students to explain how they are producing the sound using the same questions used to teach the consonants and vowels. When practicing, ask the questions randomly, out of order. You can also say a word, then ask which letter is in the beginning, middle, or end of it. Use these sounds to create a list of words to spell, read, or play games with. Sample words from this lesson might include:

pit	pat	tip	top	tap	pup
pig	tag	got	kit	kid	big
dot	bog	bag	big	pad	dab
pat	pod	pot	bet	beg	bag
tug	peg	pet	dug	keg	bit

8. Be sure that your students also understand the meaning of each of these words. Using pictures as examples, ask students to define the words and say how they could be applied to school or home activities. You can also ask what category the word belongs in—perhaps an action, object, or animal.

9. Using the Single Vowel Staircase and cards with the single consonants that have been taught, place one consonant in front of the vowel and one after the vowel, then ask students to read the word. Move the cards down the staircase to make new words, and have students read the words (pig, peg, pag, pug, pog, etc.).

All of the exercises above help create strong associations with the letters and their sounds.

Checklist for Concepts to be Taught about Sound/Symbol Correspondences

✔ There are two types of letter/sounds in the English language: consonants and vowels.

✔ Consonants come in pairs and in groups of two or three letters.

✔ Consonant pairs have one voiced and one unvoiced member. The partners in the consonant pairs are formed using the same part of the mouth, in the same location and the same flow of air.

✔ Vowels are formed by coordinating the jaw, tongue, and lips.

✔ Consonants are closed sounds.

✔ Vowels are open sounds.

✔ Every word must have one vowel per syllable.

✔ Consonants can be labeled by linguists based upon the type of air used to form them: stops, fricatives, affricatives, sibilants, nasals, laterals, and semivowels.

✔ Single consonants, consonant digraphs, blends and clusters must be defined.

✔ Single vowels, vowel digraphs, and diphthongs must also be defined.

Phonemic Awareness Activities

Although you will hear the terms *phonological awareness* and *phonemic awareness* used interchangeably, there are differences between the two.

Phonological Awareness is a broad skill set that includes identifying and manipulating units of oral language such as words, syllables, and onset and rimes.

Phonemic Awareness includes the ability to manipulate the individual sounds in spoken words, as well as skills which allow the learner to tie the sounds in a written or heard word to letters that represent those sounds. (Kilpatrick, 2015)

Efficient phonological and phonemic awareness skills are the processing skills which are necessary and integral to learning to read and spell words thoughtfully.

This is true for all learners, regardless of their age or intelligence. You can have a gifted student with poor phonemic awareness who may struggle to thoughtfully learn to read and spell, or a developmentally delayed youngster with excellent phonemic awareness skills who will readily learn to read and spell individual words.

Phonemic awareness skills are eminently teachable, but if they are not taught explicitly, this skill set will not develop automatically over time—or independent of instruction. There are countless research studies that corroborate this.

The skills of phonemic awareness include:

- Segmenting, isolating, and identifying sounds at the beginning, middle, or end of a word.
- Blending individual sounds into words.
- The ability to substitute, add, delete, and shift sounds.

The excellent blog *Six Layers of Phonemic Awareness: Improving Students' Reading Using Their Ears* (reallygreatreading.com) contains a thorough explanation of phonological awareness and phonemic awareness. This blog also defines the six layers of phonemic awareness essential to learning to read and spell in a specific hierarchy from simplest skills to the most complex skills.

Each of your literacy lessons should contain five to seven minutes of phonemic awareness activities.

Specific activities included in the initial lessons in sound/symbol correspondence are examples of how to teach phonemic awareness. Once you have a sense of what constitutes phonemic awareness exercises, you can create your own using the sounds and letters that you are teaching in a given lesson.

Definitions of Phonemic Awareness Skills

Isolating: The ability to hear and identify individual sounds within a word. A student must hold the word in their working memory, and then note what is the first, last, or intermediate sound within that word.

- The teacher says the word *sift*, then asks the student to repeat the word to be sure the student heard the word accurately, after which the teacher might ask: "What is the first sound in the word *sift*? What is the last sound in the word *sift*? What is the second sound in the word *sift*? What sound comes after the /i/ in *sift*?"

Segmenting: Saying a whole word, pulling it apart into its component sounds, then saying the sounds one at a time.

- Have your students watch you as you say the word, ask them to repeat the word several times in order to remember it, then ask them to raise a finger to count the separate sounds within the word. Avoid elongating the word in any way, being sure to pronounce it accurately without distorting the sounds. (i.e. not *mmmmaaap)*

/map/ ⟶ /m/ /a/ /p/

Blending: The ability to hear the individual sounds in a word, then saying them with little delay between the sounds until they blend into a word.

/m/ /a/ /p/ ⟶ /map/

Adding: Attaching another sound to the beginning, end, or middle of a word or a syllable.

at ⟶ bat   spot ⟶ spots   sat ⟶ spat

Deleting: Removing a sound from the beginning, middle, or end of a word or syllable.

sit ⟶ it   slip ⟶ sip   pots ⟶ pot

Substituting: Exchanging one sound for another, with consonants only substituting for consonants, and vowels only substituting for vowels.

bug ⟶ big   mug ⟶ mush

Shifting: Taking the first and the last consonant sounds in a word or consonant blend, and changing their positions.

top ⟶ pot   steks ⟶ stesk

An excellent resource for phonemic awareness activities is *Equipped for Reading Success,* David. A. Kilpatrick (2016). This resource provides multiple lists of basic and advanced phonemic awareness activities.

Teacher – Student Learning Dialogue

Introduction

Being able to play with sounds allows us to become more independent readers and spellers. In order to read a word, you have to know what sound each letter or letter string stands for, but you must also be able to blend these sounds into a complete word.

In order to spell a word, we must hear the word, say it clearly, and pull the sounds apart to figure out how many sounds are in the word and what letters go along with these sounds. Phonemic awareness exercises help us to do this efficiently.

Teaching Hints

- Be sure to define each of the phonemic awareness skills, then name them and require your students to use the terms as well.

- Some teachers use a wall chart containing the different phonemic awareness skills along with definitions and examples.

- It is also helpful to use concrete objects to demonstrate each of the phonemic awareness skills.

Phonemic Awareness Activities

These activities are to be done orally or with letters, being sure to model and teach each type of phonemic awareness in each activity.

Isolating Sounds

What is the first sound in the word, bat? */b/*

What is the last sound in the word, bat? */t/*

What sound do you hear after the /b/ in bat? */a/*

Segmenting Sounds

The teacher says the word, then the student says each sound in the word separately while raising a finger to represent each sound.

pit	*/p/ /i/ /t/*
dot	*/d/ /o/ /t/*
tug	*/t/ /u/ /g/*
dab	*/d/ /a/ /b/*
hat	*/h/ /a/ /t/*

Blending Sounds

The teacher says the individual sounds, the students say the individual sounds, then the students pull the separate sounds together to say the whole word.

/t/ /a/ /g/	*tag*
/k/ /i/ /t/	*kit*
/p/ /o/ /t/	*pot*
/t/ /e/ /p/	*tep*
/p/ /u/ /d/	*pud*

Adding Sounds

Add /p/ to the beginning of /it/	*pit*
Add /s/ to the end of /pa/	*pass*

Deleting Sounds

Take /t/ off the end of /but/	/bu/
Take /s/ off the beginning of /sag/	/ag/

Substituting Sounds

Say "pug"	*pug*
Change the /g/ at the end of /pug/ to /p/	*pup*
Change the /p/ at the beginning of pad to /d/	*dad*

Shifting Sounds

Say "tap"

Take the first sound and the last sound in the word /tap/ and change their positions   *pat*

Take the first sound and the last sound in the word /dab/ and change their positions   *bad*

Take the first sound and the last sound in the word /bog/ and change their positions   *gob*

A Strategy for Reading One-Syllable Words

Have you ever noticed that many readers and spellers do not have a strategy for sounding out an unknown word? They tend to look at the initial consonant and/or the final consonant, and then guess at the intervening letters.

Phonological processing and phonemic awareness exercises greatly aid with changing this habit, however, these phonemic awareness skills need to be explicity applied to the process of reading and spelling words. Often, students who don't have a word attack strategy try repeatedly to sound out the word while continuing to make the same mistakes. The following strategy seems to cut into that process efficiently.

If a student is having a challenging time sounding out the word *milk*, have them initially identify the vowel by either pointing to, naming, or highlighting it.

Then direct the student to associate the letter with its sound by asking these questions:

- **Does the letter "i" tell your mouth to smile or to be open and relaxed? Is your jaw open or closed?** *For the sound of the letter "i" the jaw is quite closed, and the lips are pulled back in a smile.*

- **Let's look at the Single Vowel Staircase. Can you tell me the sound "i" makes?** */i/*

Have the student blend the vowel with the letter which follows it (*il*), and then blend these two sounds with the next letter (*ilk*).

You have now created a "rime".

Finally, have the student blend the sound that immediately precedes the vowel (*milk*).

As the student is sounding out the word, she must also decide if there are any orthographic patterns that influence the pronunciation of the word. If the word is *cent*, the student would have to remember that when the "c" is followed by "i," "e," or "y," it says /s/.

Consonant and Vowel Staircase Review Activities

 Ask your students, "What do you remember about the letters we learned in our last lesson?" Possible answers include:

- There are two types of letters in English, consonants and vowels.

- Consonants are closed phonemes.

- Vowels are open phonemes.

- The consonants come in groups of two graphemes. In each group, one consonant is voiced and one is unvoiced.

- Voiced means that my vocal cords are vibrating.

- Unvoiced means that my vocal cords are not vibrating.

- The test for voiced/unvoiced is either to put my hands over my ears, or a hand gently over my voice box to feel if the letter is voiced or unvoiced.

- Ask your students to sort the consonants into pairs, or to sort all the voiced consonants into one group and the unvoiced consonants into a second group.

- Ask your students to place the vowels in order on a staircase, with the vowel that the jaw is most closed on first step followed by a progression of the least to most open jaw and lip positions.

- Dictate the sounds. Students write each letter that corresponds to a sound on a separate card. Using these cards, play any commercial board game with students saying the sound of a letter, then identifying it as a voiced or unvoiced, a vowel or consonant before taking their turn.

- Use movement, perhaps with the teacher saying a word and students hopping on or through a hopscotch grid while saying one sound per jump.

- Create words using the letters in the current lesson by having students think up as many three-letter words as they can. Take turns, with teacher and student each substituting a consonant for a consonant, or a vowel for a vowel.

- Take a blank bingo card and write the various consonants and vowels that you have taught in the grid, then have a caller for the game either say a sound or letter name.

_____

_____

_____

_____

_____

_____

_____

_____

_____

_____

_____

_____

LESSON 2

Sound Symbol Correspondences:

"f," "v," "th," "wh," "w," "h"

Concepts

The consonants that are to be presented in this lesson are single consonants and consonant digraphs, which are groupings of two letters that represent one sound.

We will also explore the articulation features of each sound/letter group. Although the letter "w" can act as a consonant, or be paired with vowels such as "aw" and "ow," in this lesson we will only deal with "w" when it acts as a consonant.

It is also important to note that while "th" can be either voiced or unvoiced (*think* = unvoiced, *those* = voiced) and words do not contain markers which can help the reader to know which sound it will make. While maintaining flexibility, students must try to pronounce words using voiced and unvoiced pronunciations in order to ascertain which sounds like a real word.

Make this lesson as simple or as complex as you need by including or excluding linguistic terms, being sure to teach your students about single consonants and consonant digraphs. You may choose to also talk about "f," "v," and "th," being fricatives, as opposed to "wh," "w," and "h," which are labeled semi-vowels.

Teacher – Student Learning Dialogue

Introduction

In the last lesson, we talked about single vowels and single consonants, one letter, one sound. In this lesson, a new category of consonants, consonant digraphs will be learned.

Consonant digraphs are two letters that make one sound. The combined sound is totally different than the individual sounds these letters make as single consonants.

The consonants in this lesson form pairs/partners or triplets. The two consonants that form a pair or partners are grouped together because the same part of the mouth, the same action, and how air comes out of the mouth is done in the same way for both consonants in the pair. One of the consonants in the pair will be voiced, and one will be unvoiced.

Another group of consonants which will be taught in this lesson form a group of three letters that are related because you open your mouth and let the air flow out: "w," "wh," and "h" are the members of this group. These consonants are called semi-vowels, because when they are pronounced, the mouth stays in one position and air is blown out, just like when vowels are pronounced.

Now we are going to learn two new pairs of consonants where the air is very different than it was with "p" and "b", "t" and "d" and "k" and "g".

Teaching the Letter "f"

The name of this letter is "f," and it says /f/. Please repeat this sound.

- When you say this sound, what part of your mouth are you using to form the sound, your lips or your tongue? *Lips*
- Are you using both lips or just your bottom lip? *Bottom lip*
- Are your teeth inside your lips or resting on the bottom lip? *The upper teeth are resting on the bottom lip*
- Is the air coming out of your mouth in a stream or a puff? *Stream*
- Is this sound voiced or unvoiced? *Unvoiced*

Finding the Partner of "f" by Comparing "f" to "m," "s," and "v"

Let's find the voiced partner of "f". Partners use the same part of the mouth, do the same actions, and create the same type of air. One letter in the pair will be unvoiced, in this case "f" and the other partner will be voiced.

Please say the sounds /f/ and /m/.

- When you say /m/, do your upper teeth rest on your lower lip? *No*
- Is there air coming out of your mouth in a stream like /f/? *No*
- Is /m/ voiced? *Yes*

Because the answer is "no" to two of these questions, "m" is not the partner of "f".

Please say the sounds /f/ and /s/.

- When you say /s/, do your upper teeth rest on your lower lip? *No*
- Is there air coming out of your mouth in a stream like /f/? *Yes*
- Is /s/ voiced? *No*

Because the answer is "no" to two of these questions, "s" is not the partner of "f".

Please say the sounds /f/ and /v/.

- When you say /v/, do you use the upper teeth resting on your lower lip? *Yes*
- Is there air coming out of your mouth in a stream like /f/? *Yes*
- Is /v/ voiced? *Yes*

Because the answer is "yes" to all of these questions, "v" is the partner of "f".

The letters "f" and "v" are a consonant pair or partners. You use the same part of your mouth to make the sounds and the air is the same. They are different letters, and "f" is unvoiced while "v" is voiced.

Teaching the Digraph "th"

All of the consonants we have learned so far have been single consonants. The letters "th" are a digraph, two letters that make only one sound which is different than the sound of the "t" and the "h" when you see them separately.

The digraph "th" says /th/ (unvoiced). Please say this sound.

- What part of your mouth are you using to form /th/, your lips or your tongue? *Tongue*
- Is your tongue inside your mouth or sticking out between your teeth? *Sticking out between my teeth*
- Is the air coming out of your mouth in a stream like /f/ or a puff like /p/? *In a stream*
- Is this consonant digraph voiced or unvoiced? *Unvoiced*

The digraph "th" can also say /th/ (voiced). You use the same part of your mouth, do the same action and use the same air to make both of these sounds. These partners are spelled with the same letters "th". The unvoiced partner /th/ can be heard in the words *bath, thank,* or *theme.* The voiced /<u>th</u>/ can be heard in the words *the* and *those*.

Teaching the Letter "h"

This letter is the letter "h," it says /h/. Please say this sound.

- Are your lips open or closed when you say /h/? *Open*
- Is the air coming out in a stream or a puff? *Puff*
- Is it voiced or unvoiced? *Unvoiced*

The "h" is formed in a similar way to the vowels because the mouth is very open when you say /h/, and a lot of air comes out of the mouth.

Teaching the Digraph "wh"

Here is another consonant digraph, two letters that make only one sound. The sound of this digraph is different than the sound of the "w" and the "h" when you see them separately. "Wh" is unvoiced, and is pronounced as if the "h" comes first and the "w" is said second, /hw/.

This digraph is formed in a similar way to the vowels because the mouth is very open when you say /hw/.

- Is a lot of air coming out of the mouth or a small amount? *A lot!*
- Do you move your lips to say this sound or do you keep them still? *Move them*
- Is this phoneme voiced or unvoiced? *Unvoiced*

Teaching the Letter "w"

The name of this letter is "w," it says /w/. Please say this sound.

- Is a lot of air coming out of the mouth or a small amount? *A small amount*
- Do your lips move when you say /w/? *Yes*
- Is the air coming out in a stream or a puff? *Puff*
- Is it voiced or unvoiced? *Voiced*

The letters "w," "h," and "wh" are grouped together and are called semi-vowels because you exhale a lot of air when you pronounce them—just like you do when you pronounce vowels.

Activities to Stabilize the Learning of Consonants and Vowels

 You can use all of the consonant and vowel sounds that you have taught in the first lesson and in this lesson to create a list of words to spell and read or to play games with. Sample words from this lesson might include:

bet	fib	vet	bed	fit	vat	pith	hot	hat
fat	bad	fig	bath	pet	hit	wet	web	thug
fog	bud	peg	fad	gap	hip	whip	that	

You can play with some nonsense words as well:

thap	fath	thub	vap	whep

There is a Connect 4 matrix for the consonants and vowels that you have taught so far in the first two lessons in Appendix C. In order to play Connect 4 strategically, each player must identify not only the letter that goes with the sound that they want to use as the play, but they must also consider a play which enhances their chances of connecting four circles either horizontally, vertically, diagonally, or in a square.

A third consideration for picking a circle on the board would be to block an opponent's chance at connecting four circles. To make this game educationally useful, you can ask the students to:

- Identify the sound of each consonant or vowel they are playing
- Choose whether the letter is voiced or unvoiced
- Tell you what the partners of the consonants are
- Give you a word that begins or ends with the letter they are playing

You can also play a Tic-Tac-Toe game with boards that have consonants, vowels, or VC / CVC words on them.

Another excellent activity is to have your students sort the consonants based upon the dominant articulation feature(s).

Sorting Consonants	
Lips	**Tongue**
Puff of Air/Plosives	Front of the tongue or back of the tongue
Pairs of Consonants	Stream of Air/Continual
Voiced	Consonant Triplets
Single Consonants	Unvoiced
	Consonant Digraphs

Possible Answers	
Lips "p-b", "f-v"	**Tongue** "t-d", "k-g", "th-th"
Puff of Air/Plosives "p-b", "t-d", "k-g"	**Stream of Air/Continuals** "f-v", "th-th"
Voiced "b, d, g, v, th"	**Unvoiced** "p, t, k, f, th"
Single Consonants "p, b, t, d, k"	**Consonant Digraphs** "th"

Ask your students to play with rhyming words, a very abstract concept. It is helpful to graphically represent this idea to demonstrate how two rhyming words share a rime, the same vowel and final consonant(s), but not the initial consonant.

An example would be:

      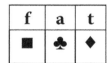

Use the following words to have your students do this exercise orally or in writing:

fog   bud   peg   fad   gap   hip   whip   that

They can create real or nonsense words that rhyme, and that have the same rime, but they must be able to distinguish between real and nonsense words. They can also use consonants that have or have not been introduced, as this is an oral activity.

Phonemic Awareness Activities

These activities can be done orally or with letters, but please remember to model and teach each type of phonemic awareness activity.

Phoneme Counting and Isolation

Ask your students to determine how many sounds are in each of these words, or in others that you choose. Give them cards with the numbers two or three on them, then after you say the target word, ask them to repeat the word, segment it, and show you how many sounds are in the word by holding up the appropriate card.

Possible Words for Counting Phonemes

at (2 sounds)	**bat** (3 sounds)	**it** (2 sounds)
add (2 sounds)	**kick** (3 sounds)	**hit** (3 sounds)
lip (3 sounds)	**peg** (3 sounds)	**bath** (3 sounds)

Identifying the Beginning, Middle or Ending Sounds in Words

thap	fath	thub	vap	whep
fat	bad	fig	bath	pet
hit	wet	web	thug	pop

Segmenting Words

The teacher says the word, the student repeats the word, then the student says each sound in the word separately, raising a finger for each phoneme.

bet	/b/ /e/ /t/
that	/th/ /a/ /t/
peg	/p/ /e/ /g/
thug	/th/ /u/ /g/
hip	/h/ /i/ /p/

Blending Sounds

The teacher says the individual sounds, the students repeat the individual sounds, then pull the separate sounds together to say the whole word

/h/ /a/ /t/	hat
/f/ /i/ /g/	fig
/p/ /e/ /t/	pet
/wh/ /i/ /p/	whip
/f/ /a/ /d/	fad

Adding Sounds

The teacher says:	The student answers:
Add /f/ to the beginning of /at/	fat
Add /th/ to the end of /ba/	bath

Deleting Sounds

The teacher says:	The student answers:
Take /g/ off the end of /fog/	/fo/
Take /v/ off the beginning of /vet/	/et/

Substituting Sounds

The teacher says:	The student answers:
Change the /b/ at the end of /fib/to /t/	fit
Change the /wh/ at the beginning of /whip/ to /d/	dip

Shifting Sounds

The teacher says:	The student answers:

Take the first sound and the last sound in these words and change their positions:

pat	tap
thub	buth
vap	pav

Use the format of these phonemic awareness activities to make up your own exercises for each day's lesson.

_____

_____

_____

_____

_____

_____

_____

_____

_____

_____

_____

_____

LESSON 3

Sound Symbol Correspondences:

"s," "z," "sh," "zh," "ch," "j," "oo"

Concepts

 The consonants and vowels that are presented in this lesson are single consonants and consonant and vowel digraphs. A digraph is a grouping of two letters that represent one phoneme, one sound. The vowel taught in this lesson is the vowel digraph "oo," which can have two sounds (as in *food* and *foot*). Each of these pronunciations is equally possible, so tell your students that when they see "oo" in a word it can be pronounced either way, and it will be up to them to decide which pronunciation is correct.

You can make this lesson as simple or as complex as you need to by including or excluding linguistic terms, but you should *definitely* teach your students about single consonants and consonant digraphs, single vowels and vowel digraphs. You may differentiate the fricatives ("s," "z," "sh," and "zh") from the affricatives ("ch" and "j").

"Zh" is not seen as an English spelling pattern, however there are a number of different ways to spell this /zh/ sound, as in bei*ge*, vi*si*on, and trea*su*re. It will be easier to talk about these spellings than to represent the sound with the letters "zh" at this time, although dictionaries direct people in the pronunciation of these various spellings with "zh".

Teacher – Student Learning Dialogue

Introduction

 This lesson introduces several single consonants and consonant digraphs that produce a lot of air when they are pronounced, and we will explore both the amount of air and whether it comes out of the mouth in a stream or a puff. We are also going to learn the new vowel digraph "oo," which can stand for two sounds.

Teaching the Letter "s"

The name of this letter is "s," it says /s/. Please say /s/.

- When you say /s/, are your lips pulled back in a smile or puckered forward? *Pulled back in a smile*

- What about the air? Is the air coming out of your mouth in a narrow stream like /f/ or a wide fan like /sh/? *A narrow stream*

- Is this sound voiced or unvoiced? *Unvoiced*

Finding the Partner of "s" by Comparing it with "ch," "sh," and "z"

Let's find the voiced partner of "s".

Partners use the same part of the mouth, do the same actions, and create the same type of air. One letter in the pair will be unvoiced, in this case "s", and the other partner will be voiced.

Please say /s, ch/.
- When you say /ch/, are your lips pulled back in a smile like /s/? *No*
- Is the air coming out of your mouth in a narrow stream like /s/? *No*
- Is the /ch/ voiced? *No*

Because the answer is "no" to all these questions, "s" and "ch" are not partners.
- Please say /s, sh/. When you say /sh/, are your lips pulled back in a smile like /s/? *No*
- Is the air coming out of your mouth in a narrow stream like /s/? *No*
- Is /sh/ voiced? *No*

Because the answer is "no" to all these questions, "s" and "sh" are not partners.
- Please say /s, z/. When you say /z/, are your lips pulled back in a smile like /s/? *Yes*
- Is the air coming out of your mouth in a narrow stream like /s/? *Yes*
- Is /z/ voiced? *Yes*

Because the answer is "yes" to all these questions, "s" and "z" are a consonant pair or partners. You use the same part of your mouth to make their sounds, and the air is the same, but they are different letters. The "s" is unvoiced while the "z" is voiced.

Teaching the Digraph "sh"

Here is another consonant digraph, two letters that make only one sound, and this sound is different than the sound of the "s" and the "h" when you see them separately: "sh" says /sh/. Please say /sh/.

- When you make this sound, are your lips pulled back in a smile or puckered forward? *Puckered forward*
- What about the air, is it coming in a narrow stream like /s/ or in a wide fan of continuous air? *A wide fan of continuous air*
- Is this sound voiced or unvoiced? *Unvoiced*

Finding the Partner of "sh" by Comparing It to "m," "ch," and "zh"

Let's find the voiced partner of "sh". Remember, partners use the same part of the mouth, do the same actions, and create the same type of air, with one of the partners being unvoiced, in this case "sh", and the other partner voiced.

Please say /sh, m/.

- When you say /m/, are your lips puckered forward like /sh/? *No*
- Is the air coming out of your mouth in a wide fan like /sh/? *No*
- Is the /m/ voiced? *Yes*

Because the answer is "no" to two of these questions, "sh" and "m" are not partners.
Please say /sh, ch/.

- When you say /ch/, are your lips puckered forward like /sh/? *Yes*
- Is the air coming out of your mouth in a wide fan like /sh/? *No*
- Is the /ch/ voiced? *No*

Because the answer is "no" to two of these three questions, "sh" and "ch" are not partners.
Please say /sh, zh/.

- When you say /zh/, are your lips puckered forward like /sh/? *Yes*
- Is the air coming out of your mouth in a wide fan like /sh/? *Yes*
- Is the /zh/ voiced? *Yes*

Because the answer is "yes" to all these questions, "sh" and "zh" are partners.

Teaching the Digraph "zh"

The spelling "zh" is not seen in words in English, but it is used in the dictionary to describe sounds in the words trea*sure*, bei*ge*, and vi*sion*. It is another consonant digraph—two letters that make only one sound—that sound is different than the sound of the "z" and the "h" when you see them separately. "Zh" says /zh/. Also, "sh" and "zh" are a consonant pair, or partners, because we create the sounds in our mouth in the same way. "Sh" is unvoiced, and "zh" is voiced.

Teaching the Digraph "ch"

Here is another consonant digraph, two letters that make only one sound which sound differently when you say the sounds separately. "Ch" says /ch/.
Please say /ch/.

- When you make this sound are your lips pulled back in a smile or puckered forward? *Puckered forward*
- What about the air, is it coming out in a wide stream or a large puff? *Large puff*
- Is this sound voiced or unvoiced? *Unvoiced*

Finding the Partner of "ch" by Comparing It to "m," "l," and "j"

Please say /ch, m/.

- When you say /m/, are your lips puckered forward like /ch/? *No*
- Is the air coming out of your mouth in a large puff like /ch/? *No*
- Is the /m/ voiced? *Yes*

Because the answer is "no" to two of the three questions, "ch" and "m" are not partners. Please say / ch, l/.

- When you say /l/, are your lips puckered forward like /ch/? *No*
- Is the air coming out of your mouth in a large puff like /ch/? *No*
- Is the /l/ voiced? *Yes*

Because the answer is "no" to two of these three questions, "ch" and "l" are not partners Please say / ch, j/.

- When you say /j/, are your lips puckered forward like /ch/? *Yes*
- Is the air coming out of your mouth in a large puff like /ch/? *Yes*
- Is the /j/ voiced? *Yes*

Because the answer is "yes" to all of these three questions, "ch" and "j" are partners. They are made with the same mouth shape and the same type of air.

Dialogue for the Vowel Digraph "oo"

The vowel digraph "oo" can have two different sounds. It is impossible to tell which sound these letters will make when you read them. You will need to learn the two possible sounds, and try to say the word using both sounds, asking yourself which pronunciation actually sounds like a real word.

- When you say the vowel /oo/ as in the word "foot," is your jaw open like /o/ or closed like /oe/? *Closed*
- When you say the vowel /oo/ as in the word "food," is your jaw open like /o/ or closed like /oe/? *Closed*
- Are your lips smiling or puckered? *Puckered*

Put your pinkie finger on your lips, then say these two sounds.

- Did your lips open or close when you said /oo/, as in "foot" and /oo/, as in "food"? *The lips close*

When you see the letters "oo" in a word, try both sounds for the vowel, then ask yourself: "Which pronunciation sounds more like a real word?"

Phonemic Awareness Activities

Isolating Sounds

Using the following list, say a word, then ask your students which letter is in the beginning, middle, or end of the word. To make this easier in a whole class setting, you can have your students create a set of cards or stickies with all of the consonant and vowel letters that you have taught so far and have them hold the corresponding card up to match the sound you say.

Saying the sound, then having students write the letter, gives them practice with sound/ symbol correspondences. You can also consider the option of having students use two different colored cards—one for consonants, one for vowels—having them write their name or initials on the back of the cards, and then store the cards in a zip-lock bag.

Teachers say these words, then ask students to show you the card that stands for the beginning, middle or ending sound:

fish	sat	pet	goop	tug
whip	wish	hop	chap	zig
zag	hoop	putt	tooth	met

Ask students to identify the beginning or ending sounds in these words:

thap	fath	thub	vap	whoop
fat	bad	fig	bath	pet
hook	wet	web	thug	pop

You can use all the consonant and vowel sounds that have been taught in the lessons up to this point to create a list of words to spell, read, or play games with. Sample words from this lesson might include:

fish	path	tooth	sit	jog	ship	zap	whop	hoop	wig
tag	gap	goop	food	fool	look	sup	shop	chap	zig

Challenge your students to make up as many words as they can with one vowel sound and the single consonants or consonant digraphs that they have learned. They can be real words or nonsense words, but the students must know the difference.

Segmenting Words

The teacher says the word, students repeat the word, and then say each sound in the word separately, raising a finger for each phoneme:

chap	/ch/ /a/ /p/
shot	/sh/ /o/ /t/
food	/f/ /oo/ /d/
sooth	/s/ /oo/ /th/
zip	/z/ /i/ /p/

Blending Sounds

The teacher says the individual sounds, students repeat the individual sounds, then pull the separate sounds together to say the whole word.

/p/ /oo/ /l/	pool
/j/ /i/ /g/	jig
/sh/ /oo/ /k/	shook
/t/ /oo/ /th/	tooth
/s/ /o/ /p/	sop

Adding Sounds

Add /sh/ to the beginning of /op/	shop
Add /sh/ to the end of /ba/	bash

Deleting Sounds

Take /n/ off the end of /toon/	/too/
Take /f/ off the beginning of /fish/	/ish/

Substituting Sounds

Change the /oo/ to /i/ in /soot/	sit
Change the /a/ to /e/ in /van/	ven

You can use the format of these phonemic awareness activities to make up your own exercises for each day's lesson.

Step Cards

Often a student will begin a complex spelling task accurately, but get lost in the middle of the process because of poor active working memory skills—the ability to hold the steps in mind as you are doing an activity.

Step cards are essentially sets of simple directions that serve as reminders of what to do for specific activities, as well as what order to do the steps in. They will assist students in being more efficient and accurate in their work.

An excellent approach is to make these learning tools with your students using age appropriate vocabulary by writing the steps on a 4"x 5" card or at the top of a page of work. Saying each step aloud for a particular skill set helps to identify and separate the steps you want to include on the card.

After you and your students have created the steps, apply them to the task at hand to make sure you haven't duplicated or left out any steps. These step cards also add clarity to your students' performance and evaluation requirements, and are helpful when they accompany homework because then both students and parents can clearly understand how and what to do for the assignment.

The step card below will help students work through a fail-safe way of spelling a word that has not been memorized. When you work with your students, ask them to spell between five and seven words in any lesson.

Spelling a Word Thoughtfully

The word you are going to spell is "stump".

Say the word aloud carefully.

Segment the word, then count how many sounds are in the word.

S T U M P = 5 Sounds

Write a dash on your paper for each sound.

— — — — —

Write a letter or letters for each sound in the word on the dashes.

<u>S</u> <u>T</u> <u>U</u> <u>M</u> <u>P</u>

Read the word once you have spelled it for accuracy.

Have your students put a copy of the step card in their spelling notebook, or tape a copy to their desk to remind them to be thoughtful when spelling words. You can also suggest they use this strategy with spelling tests.

Concentration Game

The most popular game I have ever played with my students was one Alexa Harrison Moss created a long time ago with die-cut circles containing vowel or consonant spellings on one side, and various textured cloth or wallpaper glued to the other. A match consists of finding two circles with the same textured cloth or wallpaper.

To play, all of the textured sides are turned face down, with players saying the vowel or consonant sound. Have the student identify whether it is a single vowel or consonant or a digraph before turning the piece over to reveal the colorful underside. Remember, a match is made when the backs of the cards with the designs or cloth on them are matched, *not* the letters or the words.

The game can also include Vowel plus E spellings, diphthongs, and R-controlled vowels once these vowels are taught. If a player can find two matching textured circles, he/she gets an extra turn, and the player with the most pairs of matched circles wins. The game can be played with two to four participants.

Also, when playing any game, the value is in demanding thinking and accuracy from the students when identifying the vowels or consonants. In this vein, here is a list of questions you might randomly ask your students while playing this matching game:

• Is this letter a vowel or a consonant?

• Is it voiced or unvoiced?

• What kind of air is used when you say this sound, a stream or a puff?

- Are you using your lips or your tongue to make this sound?
- If this is a consonant, what other consonant, its partner, is made the same way in your mouth?
- If it is a vowel, is your jaw closed or opened wide when you say this sound?
- Are your lips smiling, open and relaxed or closed and puckered when you say this vowel sound?
- Is this a single vowel, single consonant, or a vowel or consonant digraph?

Once your students become adept at answering your questions, ask them to be the question poser after alternating turns with you so they have many opportunities to mimic the questions you have asked. It's always best to gradually allow them to be in charge of asking all the questions, and when they can do this, they truly understand the concepts behind the skills you have taught them

LESSON 4

Sound Symbol Correspondences:

"m," "n," "-ng," "l," "r"

Concept

 The nasals and laterals are presented in this final lesson that teaches the Anglo-Saxon sound/symbol correspondences for the remaining consonants groups. All of the single vowels have appeared in previous lessons, as well as a vowel digraph for the two sounds of "oo".

The nasal consonants "m," "n," and "-ng" are given their name because either the tongue or lips block the air from coming out of the mouth, which therefore comes out of the nose when pronouncing them. The letters "m" and "n" can be used in the beginning, middle or end of a word or syllable, but the digraph "-ng" is used only at the end of a word or syllable.

Note that the digraph "-ng" is not two sounds, but is one sound produced in the back of the mouth by the back of the tongue blocking off air. The "g" is not sounded. The "n" is produced by the tongue blocking off air in the front of the mouth behind the front teeth, while the "m" is produced by the lips closing and blocking off the air.

The letters "l" and "r" are labeled laterals, and are produced by the tongue raising up and staying in contact with the palate in the front of the mouth, behind the front teeth, to create /l/. The back of the tongue raises up and stays in contact with the palate in the middle or back of the mouth to produce /r/.

When you say /r/, the front of the tongue is down on the floor of the mouth, although some individuals make the /r/ sound by using the front of the tongue and moving it farther back along the palate. Other individuals may raise the back of the tongue to produce the sound. If the sound is accurately produced, either action is acceptable. These consonants are called *laterals* because when the tongue raises up, the air comes out to the sides of the tongue.

All of the consonants in this lesson are voiced.

Teacher – Student Learning Dialogue

Introduction

This lesson introduces several single consonants and consonant digraphs that block or divert the air from coming out the front of the mouth, and we will be figuring out which part of the mouth is blocking the air. We will also review all of the single vowels and the digraph "oo" in this lesson.

Teaching the Letter "m"

The name of this letter is "m," it says /m/. Please say /m/.

- When you say this sound, where is the air coming from, your mouth or your nose? If you are not sure, gently pinch your nose and try to make this sound.

Since pinching your nose prevents you from making this sound, the air is coming out of your mouth.

- What part of your mouth is blocking the air when you say /m/, your lips or your tongue? *Your lips*
- Is it voiced or unvoiced? *Voiced*

Teaching the Letter "n"

The name of this letter is "n," it says /n/. Please say /n/.

- When you say this sound, where does the air come out, your mouth or nose? If you are not sure, gently pinch your nose and try to say /n/.

When you pinch your nose, you can't make the sound, so once again, the air is coming out of your nose.

- What part of your mouth is blocking the air when you say /n/, your lips or your tongue? *Tongue*
- The front of your tongue or the back? *The front of your tongue*
- Is it voiced or unvoiced? *Voiced*

Teaching the Digraph "-ng"

Here is another consonant digraph, two letters that make only one sound. This sound is different than the sound of the "n" and the "g" when you see them separately.

The digraph "-ng" says /ng/. Please say /ng/.

This sound is very nasal, and you do not pronounce the /g/.

- When you say this sound, where is the air coming from, your mouth or your nose? If you are not sure, gently pinch your nose and try to make these sounds.

Pinching your nose prevents you from making this sound, therefore the air is coming out of your nose.

- What part of your mouth is blocking the air when you say /ng/, your lips or your tongue? *Your tongue*
- The front of your tongue or the back? *The back*
- Is it voiced or unvoiced? *Voiced*

These two letters, "m" and "n," and the digraph "-ng," form a group called the nasals because the air is coming out of your nose instead of your lips. All of the nasals are voiced.

Teaching the Letter "l"

The name of this letter is "l," please say /l/.

- What part of your mouth are you using to produce this sound, your lips or your tongue? *Tongue*
- Are you using the front of the tongue or the back of the tongue? *Front of the tongue*
- Is the tongue lifting and staying on the roof of the mouth behind your front teeth, or is it resting on the bottom of your mouth? *Lifting and staying on the roof of the mouth*
- Is it voiced or unvoiced? *Voiced*

Teaching the Letter "r"

The name of this letter is "r," please say /r/.

- What part of your mouth are you using to produce this sound, your lips or your tongue? *Tongue*
- Are you using the front of the tongue behind your front teeth or the back of the tongue? *The back of the tongue*
- Is the back of your tongue lifting and staying on the roof of the mouth, or is it resting on the bottom of your mouth? *Lifting and staying on the roof of the mouth.*
- Is it voiced or unvoiced? *Voiced*

The two letters "l" and "r" are partners because the tongue is raised to the roof of the mouth in the front, back, or middle of the palate, forcing the air out the sides of the tongue. And "l" and "r" are called laterals.

Activities to Stabilize the Learning of Lesson 4 Consonants

 You can use all the consonant and vowel sounds that you have taught in past lessons, as well as this lesson to create a list of words to spell, read or play games with. Because the difference in sound between "m," "n," and "-ng" is so slight, it is a good idea to create some reading, spelling, fluency activities and games to highlight the differences.

The following list of words has these consonants in the initial and final positions. If you are doing this list as an auditory drill, you can use words with vowel and spelling patterns that you have not yet taught, but if you are using the list for spelling or reading, use only single vowels and "oo".

Also, if you are working with younger students or students who have inefficient phonemic awareness skills, work first with CVC words. When they are more proficient, you can use CVCC, CCVC, and CCVCC words.

mad	made	mane	boom	bum	clam
name	nod	need	nine	nip	horn
drum	mash	mile	milk	zoom	gum
long	clung	gong	song	young	mung
ban	green	ran	pen	win	fun

Words that can be used for a cumulative review during this lesson:

mood	loot	chat	lap	rap	lip
den	need	nub	not	mash	trash
him	jam	loom	room	gram	zoo
mung	nib	sung	moon	rip	ten

Challenge your students to make up words with one vowel sound and single consonants or consonant digraphs that they have learned. The words can be real words or nonsense, but the students must know the difference.

Phonemic Awareness Activities

These activities should be done orally or with letters. Be sure to model and teach each type of phonemic awareness activity.

Segmenting Words

The teacher says the word, students say the word, then students say each sound in the word separately.

mood	/m/ /oo/ /d/
mung	/m/ /u/ /ng/
soon	/s/ /oo/ /n/
ten	/t/ /e/ /n/

Blending Sounds

The teacher says the individual sounds, students says the individual sounds, then students pull the separate sounds together to say the whole word.

/t/ /oo/ /th/	tooth
/s/ /u/ /ng/	sung
/p/ /oo/ /l/	pool
/t/ /u /g/	tug

Adding Sounds

The teacher says:	Students answer:
Add /m/ to the beginning of /at/	mat
Add /n/ to the end of /te/	ten

Deleting Sounds

The teacher says:	Students answer:
Take /ng/ of the end of /mung/	/mu/
Take /n/ off the beginning of /noon/	/oon/

Substituting Sounds

The teacher says:	Students answer:
Change the /d/ at the end of /mood/ to /n/	moon
Change the /r/ at the beginning of /rap/ to /l/	lap

Playing Checkers

Place stickers on individual checkers that contain either a consonant, a vowel, or words from the lists above. Have each player read the letter(s) or the words before moving their playing piece. One way to make the game more flexible is to have a stack of cards with the skills you are working on reinforcing, having each player pick a card, then read the word or say the letter before making a move.

You can also make a sheet with the various words that you have taught so far which can be duplicated on two different, heavier weight pieces of colored paper or card stock, and cut these out to use for playing checkers. (See Appendix E)

Part III

One–Syllable Orthographic Patterns

One-Syllable Orthographic Patterns

There are two main categories of spelling patterns, which I refer to as the *Position Patterns* and the *Protection Patterns*.

The Position Patterns are based upon two factors:

- Whether a target sound occurs in the beginning, middle, or end of a word or syllable (examples include "au-aw", "ou-ow", "y").

- The second factor focuses on the fact that there is often a relationship between a target letter and the letter that directly follows it, as in the C, G, and R-controlled Vowels or one letter past the target letter, as in the Vowel plus E rule.

The Position Pattern lessons for vowels include the Vowel plus E, R-controlled Vowels, "au-aw", "oi-oy", "ou-ow", "-awl, -awn, -owl, -own", and Two Vowel Friends lessons.

Position Patterns for the consonants include the "c," "g," "x," "y," and "qu" lessons.

The Protection Principle rules are based upon the fact that the sounds of single vowels are often changed by consonants or vowels that follow them in a word. In order to maintain or not change the sound of the single vowels, more than one consonant letter is positioned after the single vowel in one-syllable words.

The Protection and Position Pattern lessons include Defining Weak and Strong Vowels, the FLoSS Rule, K/Ck Rule, Ch/Tch Rule, Ge/Dge Rule, and the Most Kind Old Pink Things Rule.

There is a handy chart on the *Spelling Cards* page at the end of this section that contains all of these spelling patterns.

_____

_____

_____

_____

_____

_____

_____

_____

_____

_____

_____

Consonant and Vowel Categories in Simple and Complex One-Syllable Words

Concepts

 Calfee et al. (1981) state in their research that all consonants and vowels fall into the following categories:

- Single Consonants
- Consonant Digraphs
- Vowel Digraphs and Diphthongs
- Single Vowels
- Consonant Blends
- R-controlled Vowels

Remembering and understanding the ideas that organize graphemes into these six categories helps to order almost 200 isolated letter patterns represented in most basic readers, and makes remembering the letter/sound patterns much easier.

Letter/sound mapping, one of the key skills that we want to teach our students, is the idea that each sound in a word is represented by one or more letters, and that those letters can be single consonants or single vowels, consonant or vowel digraphs, R-controlled Vowels, and vowel diphthongs. Consonant blends are two letters that represent two sounds, and consonant clusters are three letters that represent three sounds.

This lesson, designed to assist you in building a vocabulary for talking about the sounds and letters in word, will review the definitions of single consonants and vowels and introduce the idea of consonant blends. Two excellent resources for further information about phoneme-grapheme mapping are David Kilpatrick (2016) and Kathryn Grace (2007).

When mapping single consonants and vowels, one letter represents one sound:

pat = p̲ a̲ t̲

Consonant blends are two-letter spelling units where each letter retains its sound, so consonant blends represent two distinct sounds and letters:

stop = s̲ t̲ o̲ p̲

Sometimes students confuse consonant blends and consonant digraphs, because both are made up of two letters. Consonant digraphs make only one sound (phoneme), while consonant blends are made of two sounds (phonemes).

- Examples of Consonant Blends: "st," "cr," "pl"
- Examples of Consonant Digraphs: "sh," "ch," "ph," "wh"

When mapping consonant digraphs, the two letters of the digraph are treated as one unit of sound:

when = w̲h̲ e̲ n̲   mash = m̲ a̲ s̲h̲

Teacher – Student Learning Dialogue

 ### Introduction

We have studied several different kinds of consonants and vowels, but there are actually six categories that all consonants and vowels can be sorted into. Today we are going to review the categories we have already learned, and then we will learn a new category of consonants.

Here is a word: "mash"

- How many sounds are in this word? *Three sounds*
- What is the first sound, and which letter goes along with that sound? */m/, "m"*

The letter "m" is a single consonant, which is one letter that makes one sound.

- What is the second sound in the word "mash", and what letter represents that sound? */a/, "a"*
- Is the letter "a" a single consonant or a single vowel? *It is a single vowel*
- Can you define a single vowel? *A single vowel is one vowel letter that makes only one sound*
- What is the last sound in the word "mash", and what letters stand for that sound? */sh/, "sh"*
- Is "sh" a single consonant or a consonant digraph? *"sh" is a consonant digraph*
- What is the definition of a consonant digraph? *A consonant digraph is two consonant letters that make one sound*

Let's look at another word: "slip"

- How many sounds are in this word? *Four*
- In the word "slip," are the first two letters consonants or vowels? *They are both consonants*

The only time we have seen two consonants sitting next to each other, they have been consonants digraphs, two letters making one sound.

- When you say "slip," do the "s" and the "l" make one sound or two? *Two*

Now let's learn a new category of consonants, "consonant blends," which includes the letters "sl".

A consonant blend is made up of two consonant letters that both make a separate and distinct sound. They are made up of two consonant letters sitting right next to each other with no vowels between them.

How are consonant blends and consonant digraphs the same? *Consonant blends and consonant digraph are two letters*

How then are consonant blends and consonant digraphs different?

Consonant blends make two different consonant sounds, while the letters in a consonant digraph make only one sound, and they are different than the sound both its constituent consonants make when they are not next to each other.

Once students understand the concept of consonant blends, teach them the difference between simple and complex one-syllable words using the following dialogue. Be sure to have them look for patterns, rather than telling them the defining attributes of these words.

This list of words will help your students discover the consonant and vowel patterns in different one-syllable words:

I	my	ask
a	be	sky
at	met	glad
us	ship	last

Ask your students to label each letter in these words as a consonant (C) or vowel (V).

- **What is the same in each of these words?** *They all have only one vowel sound*

- **Do all of these words have consonants?** *Almost all of the words have consonants before or after the vowel, but a few words are made up of only a vowel.*

- **What is different about these words, do they have single consonants, consonant digraphs or consonant blends?** *Some of them have a single consonant before and/or after the single vowel letters. Some of them have consonant blends and consonant digraphs before or after the vowel*

You can summarize by explaining that a one-syllable word must:

- Have a single vowel sound, and the vowel can have consonants before and/or after the vowel sound.

- When these consonants are single consonants or consonant digraphs, the word is labeled a **simple one-syllable word.**

- When the word has one vowel, consonant blends, and single consonants or digraphs surrounding it, it is labeled a **complex one-syllable word.**

Activities to Reinforce and Distinguish Concepts of Consonant Blends and Digraphs

 Here is a list of consonant blends and digraphs. Consonant blends can be initial blends at the beginning of a word or syllable or final blends at the end of a word or syllable.

Print these letter combinations on the board or an overhead, placing the definition of consonant blends and digraphs at the top. Have students tell you which category they should put these letter combinations in or by raising a card that is labeled *blend* or *digraph*.

wh	st	cl	ch	fl	sh
sp	-pt	th	tr	shr	-ng

Only certain consonants can be combined to make consonant blends, and the most popular letters in the second position of an initial consonant blend are "l" and "r". The letter "t" is a close third for use in forming consonant blends.

Examples of these first two letters combining are: "bl," "cr," "cl," "dr," "fl," "fr," "gl," "gr," "pl, "pr," "wr".

The letter "t" often combines to make final consonant blends that come at the ends of words: "-ct," "-ft," "-lt," "-nt," "-pt," "-st".

Have your students read and spell the consonant blends, as well as words that have consonant blends. You can also make up a fluency list with the various consonant blends, digraphs, and single consonants, and have your students read them for accuracy and rate.

Laura Toby Rudginsky and Elizabeth C. Haskell (1985) offer an extensive list of initial and final blends and consonant digraphs.

Phonemic Awareness Activities

 Segmenting, blending, and analyzing sound changes in complex one-syllable words that have consonant blends is seriously important, as they are the most challenging discrimination task when reading and spelling. Be sure to practice this often, using the step card for spelling words in order for your students to make phonemic analysis and spelling a habit.

Isolating Phonemes

Ask students to identify the first or second sounds in the initial and final consonant blends in these words:

stopped	flood
trips	slush
plots	plump

Segmenting Words

The teacher says the word, students repeat the word, then say each sound in the word separately, raising a finger for each phoneme.

stop	*/s/ /t/ /o/ /p/*
trip	*/t/ /r/ /i/ /p/*
chirp	*/ch /r/ /p/*
plot	*/p/ /l/ /o/ /t/*
flood	*/f/ /l/ /u/ /d/*

Blending Sounds

The teacher says the individual sounds, students repeat the individual sounds, then put the separate sounds together to say the whole word.

/p/ /l/ /a/ /n/ /t/	*plant*
/f/ /r/ /o/ /g/	*frog*
/m/ /i/ /l/ /k/	*milk*

Adding Sounds

Add /l/ after /s/ in "such"	*sluch*
Add /t/ after /s/ at the end of /las/	*last*

Deleting Sounds

Take /t/ off after /s/ in the word "stop"	*sop*
Take /n/ off before /t/ in the word "mint"	*mit*

Substituting Sounds

Change /oo/ to /i/ in "spit"	*spoot*
Change /l/ to /t/ in "slip"	*stip*

Make a list of simple and complex one-syllable words, then have your students sort them and explain why they put each word into one category or the other.

Here are some possible words to use for your list:

blush, slush, plot, pan, red, prop, whip, plump, than, shut, chimp, nut, jam, brim, crunch, wet, brag, slip

Another useful activity is to take a list of words and ask your students to label each consonant and vowel within the word.

SC = single consonant
CD = consonant digraph
CB = consonant blend
SV = single vowel
VD = vowel digraph

chip

ch	i	p
CD	SV	SC

clash

cl	a	sh
CB	SV	CD

plump

pl	u	mp
CB	SV	CB

One-Syllable Position Patterns: Vowels
Vowel plus E Orthographic Pattern
Frequency - 3954 words

Concepts

Consonants are, for the most part, very consistent and dependable. Vowels, however, are more changeable, and in the English language vowels are involved in many different orthographic patterns. The letters that follow a single vowel change its sound, so a single vowel can be pronounced several ways. Thankfully there are some very reliable patterns that can help your students easily read and spell thousands of words.

When a single vowel is followed directly by an "e" or is followed by a single consonant or consonant digraph and then an "e", the "e" acts as a marker by changing the sound of the preceding single vowel.

In this case, the job of the "e" is to make the preceding vowel say its letter name, and this is the definition of Vowel plus E.

When making the preceding single vowel say its letter name, an "e" can reach over a single consonant or consonant digraph to influence the preceding single vowel, but cannot reach over two single consonants.

Teacher – Student Learning Dialogue

Introduction

During this lesson we will be exploring a group of vowels that have a common marker. When a single vowel letter is followed by a single consonant sound followed by the letter "e," the "e" has the special job of influencing the first vowel's sound. Let's look at some words to see if we can figure out this spelling/sound pattern.

Here are some possible words and sample questions to use to teach this rule. Be sure to point to each word as you read it for your students.

tap / tape   bit / bite   hop / hope   us / use   met / meet

Please repeat these words: "tap," "tape".

- How many sounds are in each of these words? *Tap has three sounds, tape has three sounds*

Let's put three lines on a paper to show that the word "tap" is made up of three sounds.

Please write the first sound/letter on the first line, the second sound/letter on the second line, and the third sound/letter on the third line. Do the same for "tape".

The Vowel plus E should be on one line (t a-e p vs. t a p) or the "e" can be written after the last line, showing that it comes at the end of the word, but is not making a sound, <u>t a p</u> e.

When the sound /ae/ is written in a real word, the "e" sits one consonant sound away from the "a" and can reach over that one consonant sound to tell the single vowel to say its letter name, or long sound.

Proceed through the list you are using for this lesson, saying the words, then having your students repeat the words, segment the words, and represent the sounds with slash marks or boxes.

When you say the words, be careful not to elongate or segment the word in any way, but rather pronounce it as naturally as possible. Let your students do the segmenting work.

Each of these words has three sounds, but some of the vowels are spelled with more than one letter.

- **What is the vowel sound in each word? Color the vowel sound red or underline it.** *"a," "e," "i," "o," "u," "ae," "ie," "oe," "ue," "ee"*

- **What is the same about each word in each pair?** *Each word in the pair has the same consonants, and shares a common vowel letter*

- **Is the vowel sound the same in each word within the pairs or is it different?** *One of the words in each pair has an extra vowel letter, an "e". The vowel sound in each pair is different.*

- **Does the "e" sit right next to the single vowel letter or next to one letter after it?** *In all the words except "meet," the "e" sits one consonant away from the single vowel. In the word "meet," the two letters "e" sit next to each other. Sometimes an "e" sits next to another "e," and sometimes it is separated by one consonant sound*

When a single vowel is followed by a single consonant or a consonant digraph and the letter "e" that "e" is a marker, because the job of "e" is to make the preceding single vowel say its letter name. That "E" is not making any sound.

A fun way to think about this is to say that the marker "e" can jump over one consonant sound and hit the vowel on the head, commanding it to "say your letter name". We can call that "e" a "Bopper E" or Vowel plus E.

The "e" has the strength to jump over a single consonant or a consonant digraph, but not over two single consonant letters.

bathe   taller

Activities

 Here is a list of simple and complex, one-syllable words that you can use with the activities that follow.

fade	craze	vase	brave	mate
lame	flame	wave	maze	shame
blame	these	white	wipe	crime
theme	while	grime	chime	here
file	smile	ripe	shine	chase
close	robe	stroke	hope	rove
mule	use	fuse	cure	pure
hike	feet	theme	poke	cope

Dictate these words and have your students write them on cards. Use a commercial board game and play the game according to its regular rules, but before the student can move, they must pronounce a word from the stack of words. A nice twist to this is that they take a double move if they can create a word that rhymes with whatever word they pulled from the stack of Vowel plus E words.

_____

_____

_____

_____

_____

_____

_____

_____

_____

_____

_____

_____

_____

R-controlled Vowels Orthographic Pattern
Frequency - 3751 words

Concepts

 This vowel pattern deals with each of the single vowels followed immediately by the letter "r," which is a very powerful marker because it affects the sound of each single vowel (an example of the Position Principle).

There are two distinct groups of sounds within the R-controlled Vowels, with "ir," "ur," and "er" all having the same sound of /r/, while "ar" and "or" have different sounds. Each of the single vowels changes their sound when followed by "r".

Teacher – Student Learning Dialogue

 ### Introduction

Today we are going to look at a new vowel pattern that involves single vowels and the letter "r". We will be paying attention to where the "r" sits in the word, and what its linguistic job is.

Ask the students to look at these pairs of words, then answer the following questions. Be sure that you, the teacher, pronounce the words instead of holding the student accountable for reading words and patterns that you have not yet taught.

had, hard

- When you say the word "had," what is the vowel sound? */a/*
- When you say the word "hard," does the "a" still say /a/, or has that sound changed? *Changed*
- Does the "r" come before or after the letter "a"? *After*

When the single vowel "a" is followed by the letter "r," together they are a vowel digraph, and the sound that "ar" makes is /ar/. The "r" is a very powerful letter.

pot, port

- When you say the word "pot," what is the vowel sound? */o/*
- In the word "port," does the "o" sound still say /o/ or /or/? */or/*

In the word port "or" is a vowel digraph and the sound of "or" is /or/.

gem, germ

- In the word "gem," what is the vowel sound? */e/*
- In the word "germ," does the "e" sound still say /e/, or does it say /r/? */r/*

cub, curb

- What is the vowel sound in the word "cub"? */u/*
- In the word "curb," does the "u" still sound like /u/, or does it sound like /r/? */r/*

flit, flirt

- What is the vowel sound in the word "flit"? */i/*
- In the word "flirt," does the "i" still say /i/, or does it say /r/? */r/*

The vowel digraphs "ir," "ur," and "er" all say the same sound, /r/.

When the single "e," "i" and "u" are followed by an "r," that "r" always changes the vowel sound. The "r" is a very powerful letter.

Summarize this rule for your students by saying:

When an "r" immediately follows a single vowel, the vowel sound is always changed. "ir," "ur," and "er" all say the same sound, /r/, while "ar" and "or" have different sounds. The single vowel and the "r" are a vowel digraph.

Activities

 Often students confuse R-controlled Vowels and consonant blends that are spelled with the consonant "r". An excellent activity is to have the students identify and highlight the position of the letter "r" in various words before or after the single vowel, and then sort the words based upon whether the "r" is acting as a consonant or a vowel. This list of words works well for this activity:

ramp	bird	crop	mark	drive	lurk
drug	hurl	droop	lark	cramp	hurt
grab	smirk	grid	turn	graze	jar
broth	charm	port	brake	star	torch
broke	stork	brush	term	bride	clerk
trace	first	verb	park	third	trash
tramp	fern	pride	prune	trade	sir

Another activity would be to "map" the sounds in each word, using lines to represent the sounds.

prod = p r o d   port = p <u>or</u> t   brat = <u>b</u> r a t   bart = <u>b</u> <u>ar</u> t

A sort can focus the students on the sound of the R-controlled Vowels. Sort the words into the following categories: /ar/, /or/, /r/.

Here is a list of words to use for this:

darn	hard	first	verb	burn	cork
churn	chart	clerk	port	lurk	spark

torn	worn	thirst	ford	smirk	hurl
term	mark	stir	porch	fort	fur

Reading Words with the Letter "R"

One of the difficulties that students often have with the letter "r" is figuring out the difference between when the "r" is acting as a consonant, usually in a consonant blend, and when "r" is part of a vowel digraph, an R-controlled Vowel.

You can use this list of words wherein "r" does either of these jobs to address this situation, but feel free to create your own list as well:

brad	bard	crass	cart
dirt	drop	fort	front
grunt	harm	jerk	first
lurk	murky	park	surf
strip	start	truck	turn

Ask the students to highlight the "r" with the color green when it is part of a consonant blend, because an initial consonant blend sits at the beginning of a word or syllable.

Ask your students to highlight the R-controlled Vowel in red, because that "r" stops the vowel from saying the sound of the single vowel.

Spelling Words with the Letter "R"

A common spelling error that occurs with the letter "r" is when students are spelling a one syllable word that has an /r/ sound, but they don't know whether the sound is spelled with "r" acting as a part of the vowel team "ir, ur, er," or whether the "r" is part of the consonant blend "cr," tr," or "br". Again, practicing with that specific mistake can help to clear up their confusion.

Use a list of words that has "r" acting as a consonant blend and "r" being part of the vowel digraphs "er," "ir," and "ur," framing your students' thinking by talking about these ideas.

- Ask students to spell the word "drip".
- Then ask them if this a one-syllable word.
- Explain that in a one-syllable word, there can be one and only one vowel sound, and that the vowel sound in the word "drip" is /i/.
- Ask students if the /i/ is the vowel sound in the word "drip," will the /r/ sound be spelled as part of the consonant blend "dr" or as an R-controlled Vowel?
- Explain that it has to be spelled as part of a consonant blend because "drip" is a one syllable word which contains the sound of a vowel /i/, and there can't be two vowel sounds in a one-syllable word. The /r/ has to be a consonant.

Use the same questions to analyze the following words. When there is another vowel sound the /r/ is spelled with the consonant "r".

blur	bran	breeze	stir	brush	herd	jerk	fry
stern	press	flirt	frizz	frost	crow	crop	dry

_____

_____

_____

_____

_____

_____

_____

_____

_____

_____

_____

_____

_____

_____

_____

_____

_____

_____

_____

_____

Orthographic Pattern for Digraphs "Au" and "Aw"
Frequency - 246 words

Concepts

 When these vowel letters are strung into a digraph they say the sound /au/, as in the word "paw". When they are pronounced the jaw is very open, the lips are open and relaxed, the corners of the lips are rounded, and the tongue rests in the bottom of the mouth.

The two different spellings of /au/ are markers which tell us if the sound of /au/ is in the beginning, middle, or end of a syllable or word. If you want to spell the sound of /au/ in the beginning or middle of a word or syllable, spell it with the letters "au". If you want to spell the sound of /au/ at the end of a word or syllable, spell it with "aw". This is an example of the Position Principle.

Teacher – Student Learning Dialogue

Introduction

We have learned about single vowels, Vowel plus E digraphs, and R-controlled Vowels. In this lesson, we are going to learn about another vowel digraph, two letters that make one sound.

We are also going to learn an important principle of English orthography, the Position Principle, which teaches us that where a sound occurs in a word influences the way it is written.

I will read these words for you. Please repeat them so I am sure that you heard them correctly.

saw	jaunt
thaw	caught
vault	raw
claw	caw
straw	haunt
fault	paunch
paw	law

- What letters represent the vowel sounds in these words? *"au" and "aw"*
- Are the vowel sounds the same or different in each word? *The same*
- Is the spelling of the vowel sound the same or different in each line? *Different*
- Where do the "au" vowel letters occur, at the beginning, middle or end of the words? *The beginning or the middle*

- **Where do the vowel letters "aw" occur, at the beginning, middle or the end of the words?** *The end*
- **Can you see a pattern?** *When you hear the sound of /au/ at the beginning or middle of a word, it is spelled with "au". When you hear the /au/ at the end of a word or syllable, it's spelled with "aw".*

One of the principles of spelling, the Position Principle, states that different letters spell a sound based upon where the sound sits in the word, and "au" and "aw" are examples of this principle because both spellings say the same sound, but the spelling of that sound changes depending on where the sound is in the word.

Activities

 In order to strengthen the idea of spelling the sound of /au/ based upon its placement within a word, practice identifying where the sound occurs as an isolated task before asking your students to spell or read words independently.

There are a couple of ways to do this in a whole class or small group format by providing your students with manipulatives to demonstrate their responses verbally or non-verbally. This also gets every student involved in answering the questions, rather than just a few students answering quickly.

Either ask your students to use three different colored cards with the letters "B," "M" and "E" printed on them, or give each student a piece of paper with three lines labeled "B," "M," and "E" to designate the beginning, middle or end of a word.

_____ **B**_____ _____ **M**_____ _____ **E** _____

Here are some words to use for this exercise. Say each word one or two times, have the students repeat the words, then have the students either hold up the corresponding card or place a block on the paper with three lines to represent the sound being at the beginning, middle or end of the word.

Remember to say the words naturally, without segmenting them in any way.

raw	August	vault	draw
end	*beginning*	*middle*	*end*
haul	straw	thaw	haunt
middle	*end*	*end*	*middle*

Orthographic Patterns for the Diphthong "Ou" and "Ow"
Frequency - 213 words

Concepts

 The lips move from one mouth position to another as you say the vowel sound /ou/ for "ou" and "ow". The mouth position begins with the lips open and relaxed, the tongue flat in the mouth, and the jaw quite open. The lips then seamlessly move to a closed, puckered position as the jaw closes up, while the tongue moves from being flat in the bottom of the jaw to being back and up.

Because it is easier to feel the lips moving, question your students about how their lips are moving when pronouncing the vowels in this lesson.

The diphthongs "ou" and "ow" are another example of one sound having two spellings based upon where the sound occurs in the word. In previous lessons, we have done many activities to reinforce and build these position ideas, so be sure to bring these activities forward while adding the new ones presented in this lesson.

Teacher – Student Learning Dialogue

 ### Introduction

Today we are going to be working with the /ou/ sound. Sometimes I call this the "hurting" vowel, because saying this helps me to remember the sound.

The diphthong /ou/ is a vowel sound made by moving your lips, tongue, and jaw. I will be asking you to figure out how your mouth feels when making the sound of /ou/, which has two possible spellings.

Possible words to use to teach this rule:

out	bout	bow	bound	flour	foul
ouch	pouch	cow	chow	vow	mouth
plow	brow	bound	scout	proud	round
how	now	shroud	trout	sour	cloud

- When you say /ou/, do your lips stay in one position, or do they move from one position to another position? *They move*
- Say the sound /ou/. When you begin to say this sound, are your lips open and relaxed like /o/ or closed and puckered forward like /oo/? *Open and relaxed*
- Do they move to a closed and puckered position like /oo/ or to a smiling position like /ee/? *A closed and puckered position*

Vowels that move this way are named diphthongs.

I will read some words for you, then ask you to think about what vowel letters are in each word and how the sounds are spelled.

- **What are the vowel letters in these words?** *"ou" and "ow"*
- **Are the vowel sounds in these words the same or different?** *The same*
- **Is the spelling of the vowel the same or different?** *Different*
- **Where do the "ou" vowel letters occur in the word, at the beginning, the middle or the end?** *The beginning or the middle*
- **Where do the vowel letters "ow" occur in the word, the beginning, the middle or the end?** *The end*

The Position Principle of orthography states that different letters spell a sound based upon where the sound sits in the word. In this spelling pattern, when you hear the sound /ou/ at the beginning or middle of a word or a syllable, you will spell it with the letters "ou". When you hear the sound /ou/ at the end of a word or a syllable, you will spell it with the letters "ow".

_____

_____

_____

_____

_____

_____

_____

_____

_____

_____

_____

_____

_____

_____

_____

_____

Orthographic Pattern for the Diphthong "Oi" and "Oy"
Frequency: 161 words

Concepts

 For this vowel diphthong, "oi-oy", when you begin to say /oi/, the lips are closed tight in a puckered position, the jaw is closed, and your tongue is high in the middle of the palate.

However, that's just the beginning. While forming the sound, you glide to a second position with lips pulled back in a smile as your jaw remains closed and your tongue moves down to the bottom of your mouth. This is a diphthong – a vowel sound that is produced with a gliding action.

The second important concept for this orthographic pattern is the Position Principle, because there are two ways to spell /oi/, with "oi" used at the beginning or middle of a word or syllable (as in oil and soil) and "oy," which is used at the end of a word or syllable (as in soy and oyster).

Teacher – Student Learning Dialogue

 ## Introduction

In this lesson we are going to be learning a new vowel diphthong, as well as the letters that map onto the sounds. A diphthong is a vowel that is made in your mouth by moving your lips, tongue and jaw from one position to another. The sound we will explore today is /oi/.

Possible words to use to teach this pattern include:

oil	boil	boy	joy
foil	hoist	joint	soil
coy	void	broil	point
moist	coin	join	Roy

Say the sound /oi/.

- When you begin to say this sound, are your lips open and relaxed like /o/ or closed and puckered forward like /oo/? *Closed and puckered forward*

- When you say /oi/, do your lips stay in that position, or do they move into another position? *They move*

- Do they move to an open position like /au/ or to a smiling position like /ee/? *A smiling position*

Vowels that move this way are named diphthongs.

I will read some words for you, then ask you to think about what vowel letters are in each word and how the sounds are spelled.

- In the set of words on the board, what letters represent the vowel sounds? *"oi" and "oy"*
- Are the vowel sounds the same or different? *The same*
- Is the spelling of the vowel the same or different? *Different*
- Where do the "oi" vowel letters occur in the word, at the beginning, middle or end of the words? *The beginning or the middle*
- Where do the vowel letters "oy" occur in the word, at the beginning, middle or end? *The end*
- Do you see a pattern? *The "oi" spelling is used when the sound /oi/ is at the beginning or middle of a word, and the "oy" spelling is used at the end of a word or syllable.*

In this spelling pattern, when you hear the sound /oi/ at the beginning or middle of a word or a syllable, you will spell it with the letters "oi". When you hear the sound /oi/ at the end of a word or a syllable, you will spell it with the letters "oy". This is an example of the Position Principle.

Activities

 Here are some words to use for playing games, for dictation, and for reading and spelling activities.

boy	toy	soy	Roy	Troy
point	broil	foist	loin	joist
join	void	spoil	toil	roil
destroy	hoist	cowboy	royal	enjoy
employ	annoy	decoy	recoil	poison

One of my students' favorite commercial game, Jenga, is played by first making a tower of blocks, then one by one pulling the blocks out of the stack. The object is to not let the tower collapse, and you can add an educational twist to this exciting, intense game by writing some of the words from the last few lessons on small, rectangular stickers which you attach to the end of the blocks. Before each student makes their move, they must read the word and name the orthographic pattern(s) that it contains.

Two Vowel Friends Orthographic Pattern: Lesson 1
Frequency - 902

Concepts

 In this lesson we'll examine another orthographic pattern for long vowels, which are vowels that say their letter name. The Two Vowel Friends pattern is an alternate spelling for the Vowel plus E vowel digraphs.

The Vowel plus E spelling pattern is much more common than the Two Vowel Friends pattern—3954 words versus 902 words. The Two Vowel Friends vowels are vowel digraphs, two letters having one sound. These concepts are helpful when students have to spell words because you can ask questions like:

- Which orthographic pattern will most likely represent this sound?
- What are the possible spelling choices?
- Which is the most probable way to spell this sound?

The Vowel plus E pattern is a four times more likely way to spell vowels that say their letter name than the Two Vowel Friends spelling, thus it is the most probable way to spell the /ae/, /ee/, or /oe/ sounds.

The Two Vowel Friends orthographic pattern will be broken up into two lessons, with the initial lesson introducing the alternate vowel sounds spellings "ai," "ea," and "oa" that occur at the beginning or in the middle of words like *ail, team,* and *coal.*

The second lesson will focus on the alternate spellings of the vowel sounds in the beginning, middle, and end of words, *ail, pail, pay.* This pattern, similar to the orthographic patterns "oi-oy", "au-aw", "ou-ow", which were introduced in previous lessons, is an example of the Position Principle.

Depending on the age and depth of spelling difficulties a student experiences, you may choose to divide this into three lessons, teaching /ai/, /ay/ then /ea/, /ey/, /y/, and finally /oa/ and /ow/.

You can ask students to represent the sounds within each word with boxes or dashes, which will highlight the fact that both the Vowel plus E vowels and the Two Vowel Friends vowels are vowel digraphs.

Be sure that you, the teacher, pronounce the words, instead of holding the student accountable for reading words and patterns they have not yet been taught.

Teacher – Student Learning Dialogue

 ### Introduction

We have already learned one way to get a vowel to say its letter name, the Vowel plus E orthographic pattern, which is the most popular way to spell the letter name of a vowel.

In this lesson, we are going to learn another, less frequent way of spelling vowels that say their letter name.

I will read some words for you, then ask you to think about what vowel letters are in each word and how the sounds are spelled.

gate	gait	sail	sale
meet	meat	main	mane
pane	pain	ail	ale
Pete	peat	oak	poke
see	sea	rode	road
lode	load	lone	loan

- How many sounds are in each of these words? *Two or three*
- What letters represent the vowel sounds? *"ae," "ai," "ee," "ea," "oe," "oa"*
- Are the vowel sounds the same or different in each pair? *The same*
- Is the vowel sound spelled the same way or differently in each pair? *Differently*

There are Vowel plus E spellings and "ai," "ea," and "oa".

- Where are these vowel sounds in the words, the beginning, middle, or end? *Middle*

Summarize this rule for your students by saying:

There are several ways to spell vowel sounds that say their letter name or long sound. In the English language, the most common way is "ee", "a-e" and "o-e", the Vowel Plus E spelling pattern. The other spellings using "ai," "ea," and "oa," are called Two Vowel Friends. They are the second most common way to spell these sounds.

We call them Vowel Friends because only certain vowel pairs work this way. Many phonics books have a saying which is used to help students remember this spelling pattern: "When two vowels go a' walking, the first one does the talking".

This means that when "a" and "i" sit right next to one another in a word, the "a" says its letter name, and the "i" is silent. The same patterns hold true for the "o" and the "a" and the "e" and the "a".

It is important to note that not every vowel digraph (two letter vowels that sit next to each other and share one sound) follow this same pattern. Examples of vowel digraphs that do not follow this pattern include "au-aw", "oo" and "eu-ew".

Because these three spelling patterns work similarly, we call them Two Vowel Friends to help you remember that there are only a few pairings of vowels that work this way.

Activities

 Use the list of words from this lesson, as well as other words that follow this spelling pattern, to have the students identify the position of the Two Vowel Friend vowels at the beginning or middle of words.

Where do you hear and see the Two Vowel Friends vowels, in the beginning, middle, or end of the word? Identify which sounds in these words are represented by a single consonant, a consonant blend, a vowel digraph or a single vowel.

Examples:

"roam" = single consonant, vowel digraph, single consonant
"sheaf" = consonant digraph, vowel digraph, single consonant

roam	eat	foam	sail	roast	tweak	sheaf	oat	sneak
maid	rail	boat	ail	coach	steam	ear	chain	braid

Have the students read several words and spell others. In another lesson, have them spell the words that they read in the first presentation of this activity, then have them read the words they spelled in the first activity.

_____

_____

_____

_____

_____

_____

_____

_____

_____

_____

_____

_____

Two Vowel Friends Orthographic Pattern: Lesson 2
Frequency - 902 words

Concepts

 This is the second part of the lessons focusing on the Two Vowel Friends pattern. Part One focused on the strings of vowel letters that occur in the beginning or middle of words or syllables, while this lesson adds the strings of letters that occur at the end of words or syllables, with "ai," "oa," and "ea" used to spell the vowel sound at the beginning or in the middle of a word or syllable and "ay," "ow," "ey," and "y" used to spell the Two Vowel Friends sound at the end of a word or a syllable.

The "ey" spelling pattern is used in 43 words in the Hanna et al. (1996) study, whereas the "y" with the /ee/ sound is used in 1628 words. For this reason, you may choose to omit the "ey" spellings in this lesson and teach them using a high frequency word mapping strategy instead of part of this spelling pattern.

Teacher – Student Learning Dialogue

 Introduction

We have already learned how the Two Vowel Friends orthographic pattern can be used to get the vowel in a word to say its letter name in the beginning or middle of a word or syllable. Now we want to explore how to spell this pattern at the end of a word or syllable.

As I read these words to you, please pay attention to how the vowel sound is spelled in each word, and if it appears at the beginning of the word, in the middle of the word or at the end of the word.

ail	paint	pay	
eat	seat	many	monkey
oat	goal	snow	

- What are the vowel letters in each word? *"ai," "ay," "ea," "ey," "y," "oa," "ow".*
- Are the vowel sounds the same or different in each line? *The same*
- Are the vowels spelled with the same or different letters in each line? *Different*
- Where do the "ai," "oa" and "ea" vowel letters occur in the word, at the beginning, middle or end? *The beginning or the middle*
- Where do the vowel letters "ay," "ey," "y," and "ow" occur in the word, in the beginning, in the middle or the end? *The end*
- What can we conclude about this spelling pattern?

When you want to spell /ae/, /ee/ or /oe/ with the Two Vowel Friends spelling pattern in the beginning or middle of a word or syllable, use the spellings "ai," "ea," and "oa".

When you want to spell /ae/, /ee/, and /oe/ with the Two Vowel Friends spelling pattern in the end of a word or syllable, use "ay," "ey," "y" and "ow".

- Which other spelling patterns that you have already learned are similar to this pattern of different spellings for the same vowel sound if the sound occurs in different places within the word or syllable? *It is similar to the digraph and diphthong spellings of "au-aw", "oi-oy", "ou-ow".*

Activities

Dictate the following list of words and have students write the words on small cards.

gray	stair	spear	sneak	saint	beam
snow	foam	wait	hair	stream	pray
claim	boast	stow	scream	monkey	key
clay	soak	clean	clear	braid	bail

Once you have these cards, ask your students to do sorts, play games, and use the cards to read the words as quickly as they can. These cards can also be used for phonemic awareness activities.

_____

_____

_____

_____

_____

_____

_____

_____

_____

_____

_____

_____

_____

Orthographic Pattern for "Awn," "Awl," "Own," "Owl"
Frequency – 50

Concepts

 This spelling pattern is an exception to the usual "au-aw", "ou-ow" patterns. Usually the sound of /au/ or /ou/ is spelled with an "au" or "ou" in the middle of a word. However, when the sound of /au/ or /ou/ falls in the middle of a one-syllable word, and is followed immediately by an "l" or an "n," and sometimes "k," the most common way to spell the vowel sound is with "aw" and "ow". This pattern is found in a number of common words, so it is worth exploring with your students, and it's best to talk about the fact that these words defy the rule. Then practice them by mapping words with these patterns.

Teacher – Student Learning Dialogue

 ### Introduction

We have learned the orthographic patterns "au-aw", "ou-ow" and that "au" and "ou" are most commonly used in the beginning or middle of a word to spell the sounds /au/ or /ou/, while "aw" and "ow" are more commonly used at the end of a word or a syllable to spell these sounds.

In this lesson, we are going to see certain one-syllable words that don't follow this pattern. See if you can discover the markers that signal a different spelling pattern.

crown	owl	drawn	drawl	clown	frown
awl	lawn	pawn	dawn	fowl	fawn
hawk	shawl	awning	squawk	bawl	brown
gown	prowl	growl			

- What do you remember learning about the vowels "au-aw", "ou-ow"? What is the same about these two vowel spelling patterns? *Each pair of vowels has the same sound, /au/ or /ou/*

- What is different about these vowels, "au-aw" or "ou-ow"? *The partners in each pair are spelled differently*

- Where do you use the "au" spelling and the "ou" spelling? *In the beginning or middle of the word or syllable*

- Where do you use the "aw" spelling and the "ow" spelling? *When spelling the sound of /au/ or /ou/ in the final position in a word or syllable, use the letters "aw" or "ow".*

Let's look at the words in this lesson.

- What do you see that is unexpected with the words "bawl," "prowl," "lawn," "clown," and "hawk"? *The /au/ sound is spelled in the middle of words with "aw," not "au" and the same is true for /ou/ being spelled with "ow" in the middle, instead of "ou"*

How will we know when to use the "au" versus "aw" or "ou" versus "ow" in the middle of the word? Because English is a logical language, we can find a pattern that follows the Position or Protection Principle

- Which letter or letters follow the /au/ or /ou/ sounds in each of the words that have this new spelling pattern? *"l," "n," or "k"*

- Are there any other letters that follow the vowel or only the "l," "n" or "k"? *No other consonant letters come between /au/ or /ou/ and "l," "n," or "k"*

- Can you describe the pattern? *In words or syllables, when the vowel is /ou/ or /au/, in the middle of a one syllable word, and those sounds are followed immediately by an "n," "l," or "k," use the "aw" or "ow" spellings.*

Let's look at just a couple of more words: "round," "launch," "sound," and "paunch".

- How are these words different than the other words in this lesson? *The "n" or "l" is not the only letter following the vowel sound*

To use the "ow" or "aw" spelling in the middle of a word, "l," "n," or "k" must be the only consonant following the vowel.

_____

_____

_____

_____

_____

_____

_____

_____

_____

_____

_____

_____

"Kind Old Pink Things" Orthographic Pattern
Frequency - 179 words

Concepts

 In previous lessons, we have seen how single vowels are often affected by consonants and vowels that come after them. This is true for Vowel plus E, R-controlled Vowels, as well as Two Vowel Friends.

In this lesson, we will explore some consonant markers that affect some, but not all single vowels. Those markers will be specific final consonant blends and digraphs. The patterns explored in this lesson (summarized by the name "Kind Old Pink Things") have the ending consonant blends and digraph "-nd," "-ld," "-nk" and "-ng" that affect some, but not all, of the single vowels. The aim of this lesson is to discover which vowels are affected by these consonants, as well as creating some generalities to help us remember the patterns.

Once this exploration has been done, it is beneficial to treat these patterns as word families, generating as many words as possible by changing the initial sound using single consonants, digraphs, or consonant blends:

| old | bold | cold | fold | gold | hold | mold | sold | told |
| ink | link | sink | shrink | pink | rink | stink | wink | think |

Many students with phonological processing problems have difficulties isolating and comparing the vowel sounds in this pattern. Comparing words like pin and pink can help them to hear the vowel change its sound. A few non-words are included in the following list because there are no words that have that spelling pattern in an English word.

	"-nd"	"-ld"	"-nk"	"-ng"
A	and	bald	sank	hang
E	end	held	enk	eng
I	kind	wild	sink	sing
O	bond	bold	honk	strong
U	fund	uld	bunk	strung

The teacher must pronounce each word carefully before asking students to repeat them.

Teacher – Student Learning Dialogue

 ### Introduction

Different consonants affect the single vowel that comes before them in words. The letter "r" does this in words like "car," "bird," and "corn".

In this lesson, we are going to discover which single vowels are affected by the final consonant blends "-nd," "- ld," "-nk," and the digraph "-ng".

The Single Vowel "a"—and bald sank hang

- What is the most common sound of the single vowel "a"? */a/*
- When the "a" is immediately followed by the final consonant blend "-nd," as in the word "and," does the "a" still say /a/? *The /a/ has not changed*
- When the "a" is immediately followed by the final consonant blend "- ld," as in the word "bald," does "a" still say /a/? *It sounds like /au/*
- When the "a" is immediately followed by the final consonant blend "-nk," as in the word "sank," does "a" still say /a/? *No, it sounds like /ae/*
- When "a" is immediately followed by the final consonant digraph "-ng," as in the word "hang," does "a" still say /a/? *No, it sounds like /ae/*

Two of these three final consonant blends and the digraph -ld, -nk, -ng in one syllable words change the sound of the single vowel "a".

The Single Vowel "e"— end held enk eng

- What is the most common sound of the single vowel "e"? */e/*
- When the "e" is immediately followed by the consonant blend "-nd," as in the word "end," does the "e" still say /e/? *The /e/ has not changed*
- When the "e" is immediately followed by the consonant blend "-ld," as in the word "held," does the "e" still say /e/? *Yes, the /e/ has not changed*
- When the "e" is immediately followed by the final consonant blend "-nk," as in the nonsense word "enk," does the "e" still say /e/? *Yes, the /e/ has not changed*
- When the "e" is immediately followed by the final consonant blend "-ng," as in the nonsense word "eng," does the "e" still say /e/? *Yes*

These final consonant blends and final dgraph do not affect the sound of the single vowel "e".

Single Vowel "i"— kind wild sink sing

- What is the most common sound of the single vowel "i"? */i/*
- When the "i" is immediately followed by the consonant blend "-nd," as in the word "kind," does the "i" still say /i/? *No, it says /ie/*

- When the "i" is immediately followed by the consonant blend "-ld," as in the word "wild," does the "i" still say /i/? *No, it sounds like /ie/*

- When the "i" is immediately followed by the consonant blend "-nk," as in the word "sink," does the "i" still say /i/? *No, it sounds like /ee/*

- When the "i" is immediately followed by the consonant digraph "-ng," as in the word "sing," does the "i" still say /i/? *No, it sounds like /ee/*

All of these final consonant blends, -nd, -ld, -nk, and the consonant digraph -ng at the end of one-syllable words change the single vowel "i".

The Single Vowel "o"—bond bold honk strong

- What is the most common sound of the single vowel "o"? */o/*

- When the "o" is immediately followed by the final consonant blend "-nd," as in the word "bond," does the "o" still say /o/? *The /o/ has not changed*

- When the "o" is immediately followed by the final consonant blend "-ld," as in the word "bold," does the "o" still say /o/? *No, it sounds like /oe/*

- When the "o" is immediately followed by the final consonant blend "-nk," as in the word "honk," does the "o" still say /o/? *The /o/ has not changed*

- When the "o" is immediately followed by the final consonant digraph "-ng," as in the word "song," does the "o" still say /o/? *The /o/ has not changed*

Only one of these final consonant groups at the end of one-syllable words, -ld, change the single vowel "o".

Single Vowel "u"— fund uld bunk strung

- What is the most common sound of the single vowel "u"? */u/*

- When the "u" is immediately followed by the final consonant blend "-nd," as in the word "fund," does the "u" still say /u/? *The /u/ has not changed*

- When the "u" is immediately followed by the final consonant blend "-nk," as in the word "bunk," does the "u" still say /u/? *The /u/ has not changed*

- When the "u" is immediately followed by the final consonant digraph "-ng," as in the word "strung," does the "u" still say /u/? *The /u/ has not changed*

- When the "u" is immediately followed by the final consonant blend "-ld", as in the nonsense word "uld", does the "u" still say /u/? *The /u/ has not changed*

None of these final consonant groups at the end of one-syllable words change the single vowel "u".

Another common final blend, "-st," also affects the vowel letter "o," making it say its letter name, like in the word "most".

Reviewing the Spelling Rules

When students begin working on their spelling and reading, it is imperative that their phonological and orthographic skills be evaluated to help set learning goals.

After working with students for a school year, re-evaluate them to create a picture of their progress. Sometimes when retesting is done, mistakes students make will be puzzling, because although they have been taught concepts, they may not have retained them.

Regular review activities must be a part of each lesson plan. Spelling cards and/or tool bars can aid in those review activities to help students think about the patterns and remember them.

Teach a rule, practice it—teach another rule, and practice that one—then create activities that practice numerous rules:

- Teach Rule #1
- Practice Rule #1
- Teach Rule #2
- Practice Rule #2
- Practice Rules #1 and #2
- Teach Rule #3
- Practice Rule #3
- Practice Rules #2 and #3
- Practice Rules #1, #2, and #3

The Vowel plus E, "au-aw", "oi-oy", "oo" and Two Vowel Friends in complex and simple, one-syllable words have been taught in the previous lessons. Here is a list of words that you can use to have your students read, spell and write sentences with words, identify orthographic patterns, play games, create their own games, use as flash cards, etc.

dash	crib	romp	booth	blaze	pine
sweep	spit	cheer	skip	three	soil
brook	strive	spike	mast	hoist	fool
stump	spoil	took	shook	joint	stare
trail	strain	train	stray	sway	play
foam	soap	goal	moan	roach	roam
soak	float	show	throw	crow	elbow
stow	minnow	pillow	grow	beach	peak
bead	beak	beam	bean	bleach	bleak
cheap	cheat	clean	cream	dirty	frosty
handy	bumpy	sandy			

Activities for Practicing Spelling Patterns

1. Have students read a list of phrases or spell phrases that are based upon the current concept or pattern you are teaching or reviewing for accuracy.

2. Have students write a sentence with words that contain the patterns or current concepts that you are teaching or reviewing.

3. Give students a list of words and have them create a set of phrases or sentences using those words.

4. Make a list of words by combining the letters you are teaching or reviewing.

5. Do a visual scanning task to pick out the words that have a specific type of consonant, vowel, or spelling pattern that you are teaching or reviewing.

6. Play a Concentration game with the words, letters or spelling pattern you are teaching or reviewing by matching single consonants to single consonants, single vowels to single vowels, words with Vowel plus E, two words that have "c" = /s/ or /k/.

_____

_____

_____

_____

_____

_____

_____

_____

_____

_____

_____

_____

_____

_____

One-Syllable Position Patterns: Consonants
The "C" Orthographic Pattern
Frequency - 5731 words

Concepts

The letter "c" can be pronounced in one of two ways depending on the letter that comes after it, so this rule follows the Position Principle, with "c" saying /s/ when it is followed by the letters "i," "e," and "y". If any other letter follows "c," it will always say /k/. This is a very reliable and stable rule.

Teacher – Student Learning Dialogue

Introduction

Up until now we have learned the consonants that have one sound, except for the digraph "th," which can be voiced or unvoiced as in the words *those* and *thing*.

The single consonant letter "c," which we are going to investigate in this lesson, has two sounds. We want to find out what letters or markers signal or predict its sound in each word.

Asking your students what they already know about this spelling pattern before beginning this lesson will be an important first step.

After writing these words on cards, have your student sort them into two categories based on whether the sound of the "c" is /k/ or /s/, with the teacher reading the words out loud to the student(s)

1.	cat	cut	came	cot
2	crab	cloud	cram	cry
3.	cent	face	cycle	pencil

On the first row, what is the sound of the C? /k/

What letters immediately follow the letter C on the first row? A, O, U

What can you conclude (say) about the sound of the letter C when it is followed by the vowels A, O, or U? *When the letter C is followed immediately by the letters A, O and U it sounds like /k/.*

On the second row, what is the sound of the C? /k/

What letters immediately follow the letter C on the first row? The consonants L and R.

What can you conclude (say) about the sound of the letter C when it is followed by the consonants? *When the letter C is followed immediately by the consonant letters, it sounds like /k/.*

How to Teach Reading and Spelling: Bringing the Science of Reading into the Classroom

On the third row, what is the sound of the C? /s/

What letters immediately follow the letter C on the first row? The vowels I, E and Y.

What can you conclude (say) about the sound of the letter C when it is followed by the vowels I, E, and Y? *When the letter C is followed immediately by I, E and y it sounds like /s/.*

There has to be a reason for the different sounds that "c" makes. A marker is a letter that signals a sound change of the letter that comes immediately before it in a word. The marker in this instance comes after the targeted letter, "C".

- **What letter comes after each "c" when it sounds like /k/?** *"a," "o," "u" or a consonant like "cl" or "cr".*
- **What letter comes after each "c" when it sounds like /s/?** *"i," "e," or "y"*

This is an example of the Position Principle. When "c" is followed by an "i," "e," or "y" it always says /s/. If it is followed by any other letter it says /k/. The letter that follows "c" is a marker, it tells you what the "c" will sound like.

• • • •

Here are some other interesting facts that you can introduce to your students about the "c" orthographic pattern on subsequent days:

- Which letter is the most popular spelling of the /k/, "c" or "k"? Have students go to a dictionary and note how many pages are devoted to words that begin with "c" and with "k". What they will find out is that there are many more pages devoted to "c" words. If you look at the words that are on the "k" pages, you will see that the majority of those words have an "i," "e," or "y" as the vowel sound.

- Most words in the English language that begin with the letter "k" come from a foreign language: Kansas is Native American, kayak is Inuit and karakul is Russian.

It is also useful to create a step card for this rule with your students to help them think about how to read words with "c," as well as what to ask themselves when they have to spell words with the sounds /k/ or /s/.

Step cards for reading words that have a "c" might have the following questions on them:

> ## What letter follows the "c"?
> If the letter is "i," "e," or "y," the "c" will say /s/.
> If "c" is followed by any other letter, it will say /k/.

In order to spell a word with the /k/, you have to ask yourself:

98

> ## What is the vowel in this word?
>
> **If the vowel is "i," "e," or "y," the /k/ will be spelled with a "k".**
>
> **If a consonant follows the /k/ or the vowels is "a," "o," or "u," the /k/ will be spelled with a "c".**
>
> **By far, your best bet for spelling /k/ is the "c".**

In order to spell a word with the /s/, you have to ask:

> ## What is the vowel in this word?
>
> **If the vowel that immediately follows the /s/ in the word is an "a," "o," or "u," the /s/ will be spelled with an "s".**
>
> **If the vowel that immediately follows the /s/ in the word is an "i," "e," or "y," the /s/ might be spelled with a "c".**
>
> **If a consonant follows the /s/, then it will be spelled with an "s".**
>
> **Write the word with both a "c" and an "s".**
>
> **Which spelling looks "right" to you?**
>
> **Check the spelling of the word in a dictionary.**

The sound of /s/ at the end of a word is spelled a number of different ways: "ce," "se," "ss," depending on the vowel that precedes it. These patterns will be covered in later lessons.

Activities

1. Dictate a list of "c" words to your students and have them write the words on small cards.

2. On a different day, have them sort the words based upon whether the "c" sounds like /s/ or /k/.

3. These cards can also be used by pairs of students to play a game of War in which each player holds a stack of cards in their hand with the word side of the card facing down. Simultaneously, the players turn over a card and race to say the word or the sound of the "c" (/k/ or /s/) before their opponent can pronounce the word or sound. This activity will train the students to pay attention to the markers.

In the case of a tie, each player places three of their own cards face down on the table and reveals the fourth card, trying to pronounce the word or sound before their opponent. The first person to say the fourth word collects all four of their opponent's cards. The person at the end of the game with the most cards is the winner.

The "G" Orthographic Pattern
Frequency - 2511 words

Concepts

The letter "g" can also be pronounced in two ways, with the most frequent pronunciation being /g/ and the least frequent being /j/.

The pronunciation depends upon the letter that comes after the "g," so this is another example of a rule which follows the Position Principle. If the "g" is followed by an "i," "e," or "y," the "g" sometimes says /j/. If the "g" is followed by any other letter, it will say /g/.

Because this rule is not as reliable as the "c" rule, students must be flexible as they try out the alternate sounds and ask themselves, "Does that sound like a real word?"

Teacher – Student Learning Dialogue

Introduction

The letter "g" is another consonant that can be pronounced two different ways. In this lesson, we want to discover which markers (letters) signal each of its sounds.

Possible words to use to teach this rule include:

1.	go	garden	gun	gossip
2.	gym	age	ginger	gypsy

On the first row, what is the sound of the G? /g/

What letters immediately follow the letter G on the first row? The vowels O, A and U

What can you conclude (say) about the sound of the letter G when it is followed by the vowels O, A , or U? *When the letter G is followed immediately by the letters A, O and U it sounds like /g/.*

On the second row, what is the sound of the G? /j/

What letters immediately follow the letter G on the secondrow? I, E, and Y

What can you conclude (say) about the sound of the letter G when it is followed by the vowels I, E or Y? *When the letter G is followed immediately by the letters I, E and Y it sounds like /j/.*

There has to be a reason for the different sounds that the "g" makes. A marker is a letter that signals a sound change and the marker for this pattern always comes after the targeted letter, so we want to pay attention to the letter that comes after the "g" in each word.

This is an example of the Position Principle. When "g" is followed by an *"i," "e," or "y"* it *sometimes* says /j/. If it is followed by any other letter, it always says /g/.

The letter that follows "g" is always a marker, and it tells you what the "g" will sound like.

- Which other spelling pattern, that you have already learned, is similar to this spelling pattern? *The "c" rule*

It is important that you create graphics or step cards for this rule to reinforce the ideas to help your student read and spell words with "g" in them.

A step card for reading words that contain "g" might have the following questions on it:

- What letter follows the "g"?
- If the letter is "i," "e," or "y," the "g" could say /j/ or /g/.
- Try both sounds and listen to which word sounds like a real word.
- If "g" is followed by any other letter it will say /g/.
- The most frequent pronunciation of "g" is /g/. Therefore /g/, it is the "best bet" for pronouncing a "g" in an unknown word.

A step card for spelling words with a "g" might include the following questions:

- In this word, do you hear a /g/ or /j/?
- If you hear /g/, it will be spelled with a "g".
- If the vowel in the word is "a," "o," or "u," the /j/ sound will be spelled with a "j".
- If the vowel in the word is "i," "e," or "y," the /j/ sound could be spelled with a "j" or a "g".
- Write the word both ways, which one looks more familiar? Check yourself by looking it up in the dictionary or using spell-check on your computer.

Here are some words to practice using these step cards:

jab	gem	germ	jeep	jar	gym
jam	age	June	jig	gap	give
gave	goof	get	grate	ginger	gent

Another interesting exploration to have with your students involves a discussion of the words *guest* and *guess*. Once your students understand the "i," "e," or "y" can affect the sound of the "g," it is easy to see why the place holder "u" is used in the word *guest* or *guess*. You don't hear a sound for the "u," but it keeps the "e" from changing the sound of the "g". When working with your students, put these two words up on the board or overhead, then read them out loud and ask them, as linguists, how they might account for the "u" being in these words.

The "Y" Orthographic Pattern
Frequency - 2098 words

Concepts

 In the Hanna et al. (1996) study, the position within words, beginning, middle or end and the sounds and frequency of the letter "y" were counted. It was found that "y" most frequently resides at the end of two-syllable words, saying /ee/ in 1628 words.

A less frequent pattern in 251 words occurs when "y" is at the end of one or in multi-syllable words saying /ie/, while "y" also occurs in words of Greek origin, saying /i/ in 162 words. In each of these three instances "y" acts as a vowel. "Y" acts as a consonant at the beginning of 57 words saying /ee/.

This information is useful in teaching students to be flexible with all of the possible sounds that "y" can represent.

The pronunciation of the letter "y" in the beginning of a word is challenging for many people, since most of us have taught that it is pronounced /yu/. But if that were true, the word "yes" would be pronounced /yu/ /e/ /s/.

When we pronounce words that begin with the letter "y," we coarticulate the sounds saying them together very quickly. The "y" and the voiced vowel that follows it sounds like /ee, u/.

Because it is so hard to separate the sound of the "y" and the vowel that follows it, do not get stuck arguing for one pronunciation or the other (/ee/ vs. /ee u/) as long as students can read and spell words accurately with a "y" at the beginning of words.

Once your students understand the concept of the "y" pattern, they will be highly accurate when reading and spelling words which contain this letter.

Teacher – Student Learning Dialogue

 ### Introduction

The letter "y" is a changeling—it can act like a consonant in one position in a word, and it can work as a vowel in other positions. It also sounds differently depending upon where it is located in the word. In this lesson we want to figure out how "y" is working.

Possible words to use to teach this rule:

1.	yellow	yard	yarn	yes
2.	gym	mystery	lynch	myth
3.	my	sky	fly	shy
4.	supply	multiply	lullaby	
5.	funny	cloudy	silly	happy

Using the words on Line 1 ask your students the following questions:

- What is the sound of the "y" in beginning of words? */ee/*
- Is it working as a consonant or as a vowel at the beginning of a word? *A consonant because there are other vowels in these words.*

The letter "y" works as a consonant in the beginning of a word or syllable, and it says /ee/.

Using the words on Line 2 ask your students the following questions:

- When the "y" is in the middle of a word, does it act as a consonant or vowel? *A vowel, there are no other vowels in the word*
- What is the sound of "y" in the middle of a word? *It says /i/*

Using the words on Line 3 ask your students the following questions:

- At the end of a one-syllable word, what is the sound of "y"? */ie/*
- Is it working as a vowel or as a consonant? How do you know? *There are no other vowels in the word, so it is acting as a vowel*

Using the words on Line 4 & 5 ask your students the following questions:

- At the end of a two-syllable word, what does the "y" sound like? */ee/, /le/*
- Is it working as a vowel? *It is acting as a vowel*

It would be very helpful to create a step card for this pattern. Appropriate questions for the learner to ask might include:

- **Where does the "y" occur in this word, at the beginning, middle, or end?**
- **What are the possible sounds that the "y" could make in this word?**
- **Say the word. Does it sound like a real word?**

One way to summarize this pattern for students would be to graphically show where the "y" occurs, as well as its sound:

y _____ = /ee/   _____ y _____ = /i/

_____ y = /ie/   _____ _____ y = /ee/

Dictate a list of words that have "y" in different places, or have the students write the words on small cards. You can play many games with these cards including dominoes. Place all of the cards which two, three, or four students have written into a pile with the words facing down, then have each player take five cards out of the pile, after which they take turns playing the pieces end to end, matching words which have the same sound of "y": /ie/, /ee/, or /i/. As a player places a card, she draws another from the common pile.

The "X" Orthographic Pattern
Frequency - 398 words

Concepts

The letter "x" most frequently says /ks/ and resides at the end of a word in 350 words in the Hanna et al. study (1966).

When "x" is in the middle of a word, it can either say /ks/ or /gz/, however, there were only 43 words in the study that followed that pattern. The letter "x" can also sit at the beginning of words sounding like /z/, but this is a rare bird, with only the words like this appearing in the study: *xerox, xenon, xylophone,* and *Xerxes.*

The relative infrequency of "x" at the beginning and middle of a word suggests that these two patterns be taught only to older students. While it may be useful to expose younger students to the concept of different sounds for "x" in different positions in a word, you need not require them to spell and read words in those infrequent categories. When "x" sounds like /gz/ or /ks/, it is a single letter, but it represents two sounds. It is the only letter in English that behaves this way.

If some of your students have phonological processing difficulties, they may have a challenging time identifying how many sounds the "x" represents.

Teacher – Student Learning Dialogue

Introduction

We have learned about several different types of consonants: single consonants like "s," "b," "t," and "c," and consonant digraphs like "sh," "ch," "th," "-ng," two consonants that represent one sound.

The letter "x" is interesting because it represents a number of different sounds. Let's explore this list and listen for the different sounds it makes in the beginning, middle, and end of words. Also, since "x" can represent more than one sound, we'll find out how many sounds it represents in these words.

The sounds of the letter "x" are based on where the letter sits in the word. The most common place for it to be seen is at the end of a one syllable word. "X" says two sounds, one right after the other.

Please say each of these words:

fox	mix	six	lox	pox	sax

- What is the first sound that you hear after each vowel in each of these words? */k/*
- What is the sound that you hear right after the /k/? */s/, "x" says /ks/ at the end of a word*

The letter "x" can have two different sounds in the middle of a word. To understand the sounds of "x" in the middle of a word, we need to talk about consonant pairs, which are two different letter sounds articulated similarly, using the same part of our mouth and the same air flow, one voiced and the other unvoiced.

Let's figure out the patterns in these words together:

1. exit   exist   exam   exact
2. excite   expert   exercise

Using the words on Line 1 ask your students the following questions:
- In the word "exit," what sound do you hear right after the /e/? */g/*
- What sound do you hear right after the /g/? */z/*
- Are /g/ and /z/ voiced or unvoiced? *Voiced*

Using the words on Line 2 ask your students the following questions:
- In the word "excite," what sound do you hear right after the /e/? */k/*
- What sound do you hear right after the /k/? */s/*
- Are /k/ and /s/ voiced or unvoiced? *Unvoiced*
- Are these sound patterns /ks/ and /gz/ what you hear in all of the words on Lines 1 and 2? *Yes*

/k/ and /g/ are a consonant pair, /k/ is unvoiced and /g/ is voiced.

/s/ and /z/ are a consonant pair, /s/ is unvoiced and /z/ is voiced.

In the middle of a word, "x" says either /ks/ or /gz/.

You have to be flexible with the sound of "x" in the middle of a word. Say the sound as /ks/ and /gz/ and listen for which pronunciation sounds like a real word.

- Which spelling pattern that you have already learned is similar to this spelling pattern? *It is similar to the "y" pattern because both "x" and "y" change their sound/letter relationship based upon their relative position in the word*

It would be very helpful to create a step card for this "x" pattern which might include the following questions:

- Where does the "x" occur in this word, in the middle or at the end?
- What are the possible sounds that the "x" can make in this position?
- What is the most probable sound for "x" to make in this position?
- Say the word; does it sound like a real word?
- Be flexible, try the alternate sound possibilities.

Have older students look in a dictionary to find how many words begin with the letter "x". Since most dictionaries have only one or two pages devoted to this letter, explore the words, noting their language of origin and their meanings.

For younger students, dictate a series of words that either end with an "x" or that are multi-syllable words with "x" in the middle, then have them write these words on cards with their initials on the back of each one so two students can combine their decks of "x" words.

Place these cards in a rectangular array with the words face down to play a game of Concentration, with students saying the words on the cards that they turn over, including the sound of the "x". A match will be two words that have the same "x" sound.

The "Qu" Orthographic Pattern
Frequency - 220 words

Concepts

 The next consonant spelling pattern, "qu," is unique. Not only is it spelled with a consonant and a vowel, but the letter "q" is never seen in an English word without a "u" following it. The "u" does not act as a vowel here, it is a part of the "qu" pattern. Whatever syllable "qu" resides in will have another vowel sound.

The spelling pattern "qu" is usually found at the beginning of words, where the two sounds it represents are /kw/, and a less frequent use of this spelling pattern occurs at the end of words derived from French, such as antique, mystique, and grotesque. This is a rare pattern where the "que" says /k/.

When teaching young children, only present the first of these two ideas, but when teaching students in fourth grade or above, you can teach the French pattern in a separate lesson.

Teacher – Student Learning Dialogue

 ### Introduction

The spelling pattern "qu" is a novel one, because "u" usually acts as a vowel. However, when "q" and "u" are paired, the "u" will not act as a vowel, rather "q" and "u" work as a consonant team. You will never see an English word with a "q" not followed immediately by a "u".

Let's listen for the sounds that "qu" makes in the following words, please repeat each word after me:

quick	quite
quake	quote
queen	quit

- What letter immediately follows the "q" in each of these words? *"u"*
- Is there another vowel sound in each word? *Yes*

When "q" is found in an English word, it is always followed by the letter "u".

Remember, "u" is not acting as a vowel. There will always be another vowel sound in the word.

- What is the vowel sound in each of these word?
- In each of these words, what is the first sound that you hear? */k/*
- What is the second sound? */w/*

"Qu" does not have a sound of its own, its sounds are /kw/.

Students who have phonemic awareness difficulties often cannot perceive both of the sounds "qu" makes, and the following dialogue may help them to discover both the /k/ and the /w/ sounds.

If your students say the "qu" in the word quick says only /k/, respond by saying:

You told me that the word *quick* **says** *kick***. What sound do you hear after the /k/ in /kwik/?** */w/*

Alternately, if the student says "qu" says /w/, respond by saying:

You are telling me that the word *quick* **says** *wick***. What sound do you hear before the /w/ in /kwik/?** */k/*

The French "-que" Orthographic Pattern
Frequency - 220 words

Concepts

The English language is a mixture of words borrowed from many languages, with French words entering into the English vocabulary when the Norman French invaded England in 1066 and donated approximately 10,000 words to Middle English.

Many multi-syllable words that middle school, high school, and college students encounter which derive from the French language have unique spelling patterns, and therefore should be explored with older students. A common pattern has "-que" as an ending spelling, and these letters say /k/.

Because these words are not seen frequently in texts, the concept can be taught, and then reviewed, as words occur in the students' reading and writing experiences. A helpful strategy to use in this case is a mapping technique that will highlight the regularity of most of the sounds in each word, as well as the unpredicted sounds.

Teacher – Student Learning Dialogue

Introduction

The letter combination "qu" has been taught as a consonant team because "q" is never used in English words without a "u" following it, and it represents the two phonemes /k/ and /w/.

In this lesson, we will be exploring words that come from the French language, which English has adopted. Think about what the sound of "qu" is in each of the following words, and where these letters sit in the word, the beginning, middle or end.

antique	picturesque
clique	technique
grotesque	unique
mosque	oblique

- In each of these words, what letter immediately follows "qu"? *"e"*
- Where does "-que" usually sit, in the beginning, middle or end of the word? *The "-que" comes at the end of the word*
- Let's map the sounds of this word onto dashes. How many syllables are in each word? One or two? *One and two _____ or _____ _____*
- Please make one or two large lines on a piece of paper to indicate if the word is a one- or two-syllable word.
- Let's work on the word antique. Is it a one- or two-syllable word? *Two*

- Make two large lines on a piece of paper to represent the two syllables in the word, antique.
- How many sounds are in each syllable? *First syllable, two sounds,second syllable three*
- Please put two shorter lines above the long line that designates the first syllable and write the letters that stand for the sounds in the first syllable.

  a   n

  _____   _____

- How many sounds are in the second syllable? *Three*
- Please put three shorter lines above the longer line that designates the second syllable, then write the letters that stand for the sounds in the second syllable.

  a   n   t   i   que

  _____   _____

- What sound does the "i" represent in each of these words? */ee/*
- What sound does the "que" represent in each of these words? */k/*
- Can you summarize or define this "-que" spelling pattern in your own words?

  In words that are borrowed from French, in the last syllable the "qu" is always followed by an "e" and sounds like /k/. The "-que" often has an "i" before it, and together "-ique" says /eek/

Be sure to explore the meanings of all these words with your students, and have the students use them in oral sentences. Find synonyms and antonyms, and perhaps even find out their etymological history (i.e. antique *is from Middle French, and the Latin* antiquus, *which means "in front," "existing earlier," and "ancient",* clique, *also from Middle French, which means "to make noise").*

Obviously, words like mosque *and* mosquito *derive from languages other than French, but seeing how and when words have entered English can be interesting to the budding linguists in your class.*

_____

_____

_____

_____

_____

_____

_____

One-Syllable Protection Patterns

We have explored the Position Principle with lessons like the "C" rule and the "oi-oy" spelling patterns. A second important group of spelling rules comes under the category of the Protection Principle, with spelling patterns based upon the vowel in a word.

Single vowel sounds are easily influenced by other vowels, and even some consonant letters. Because of this, the Single Vowels are dubbed *weak* vowels for the purposes of these lessons.

Weak vowels can be protected by two or more consonant letters following the vowel which maintain that vowel sound. Two adjacent consonants located after a single vowel "protect" the vowel from being influenced by ensuing vowels.

If you have a *strong* vowel in a word, a vowel spelled with two letters ("ai," "ou," "ar," "oi") the ensuing consonants are spelled differently because you don't have to protect the vowel sound. Examples of this include:

fusses / fused   pitches / pooches

milked / mill / mile   picked / pike

The spelling patterns that are categorized under the Protection Principle are:

The Floss Rule   The K/Ck Rule

The Ge/Dge Rule   The Ch/Tch Rule

The Doubling Rule

Both the Position and the Protection Principles explain these spelling patterns.

_____

_____

_____

_____

_____

_____

_____

_____

_____

_____

_____

Defining Weak and Strong Vowels

Concepts

 The terms short and long vowels were established long ago and knowing the history and evolution of the English language will help in understanding what these terms mean.

In Old English, there were single vowel letters, "a," "e," "i," "o," and "u". In some words the vowels were pronounced for a short duration of time, and the same vowels could also be pronounced for a longer duration of time, hence the names *long* and *short* vowels.

The meanings of the words differed based upon the duration of pronunciation of the vowels. As the English language evolved, the vowels and the letters that represented them changed.

One major change in vowel pronunciation occurred during the Middle English period, which came to be known as "The Great Vowel Shift". The spelling patterns for vowel digraphs and diphthongs reflect this variation.

Although the terms short and long vowels are still used today, they are an anachronism. Students are often confused about the meaning of these labels because the meaning of these words no longer reflects the sound qualities of the vowel sound.

However, the labels **weak** and **strong** are meaningful because the term captures the idea of the interaction of the vowels and the spelling of the letters that come after them.

A **weak** vowel is a single vowel, while **strong** vowels are digraphs or diphthongs. The sound of a single letter vowel can easily be changed by other letters that directly follow it.

If another vowel comes after the single vowel, it is no longer a single vowel and its sound changes—as in "au" and "oi". If specific consonants follow the single vowel, its sound will also change, as in "or," "ing," "old," and "all".

It is because single vowel sounds are so easily changed by other letters that they are dubbed **weak**. To maintain the single vowel's sound, it must be followed by two or more consonants to be protected or preserved.

Digraphs and diphthongs are not changed by the letters that follow them, and because their sounds don't vary, they are labeled **strong** vowels.

Many orthographic rules in English have two possible letter combinations or spellings that can be used at the end of a word or syllable. The sound of /k/ can be spelled with "k" or "ck", at the end of a word or syllable /ch/ is spelled with either "ch" or "tch", and at the end of a word /j/ is spelled with either "ge" or "dge".

The factor that determines which string of letters will be used to spell these sounds at the end of a word is the type of vowel in the syllable or word. We use "tch," "ck," and "dge" to protect a **weak** vowel with two consonants. With a **strong** vowel, a digraph or diphthong, "ch," "k," and "ge" are used.

The key concept we are teaching here is that a single vowel is highly changeable, and the letters that come after it can maintain or change its sound.

The focus of this lesson is on teaching our students how to maintain the sound integrity of a single vowel. In order to truly think through the ideas in this lesson and to answer the questions accurately, students must have already learned and integrated other orthographic patterns: single vowels, Vowel plus E, digraph and diphthong sound/letter patterns, and the R-controlled vowels.

Teacher – Student Learning Dialogue

Introduction

Weak and strong vowels are a critical concept of the Protection Principle, but what does the word *weak* mean? What does the word *strong* mean? What does the word *protection* mean? *Elicit definitions from your students for these three terms.*

We are going to use the following words to help us understand some new spelling patterns after we review previously learned vowel sounds by sorting them into categories:

bat	bar	rate	taunt	sank	ball
met	sister	meet	meat		
got	pork	pole	pooch	pouch	point
pit	birth	pile	sing		
cut	curt	cute			

- **What are the vowel letters in each of the words on the first line?** *"a," "ar," "au," "ae"*

- **What is the same about all of these vowel letters?** *They all have the letter "a"*

- **When there is the single vowel "a" in the word bat, what is the sound of that letter?** */a/*

- **When you pronounce the word "bar," do you still hear the /a/ sound? What is the sound of "ar"?** *No, /ar/*

- **When you pronounce the word "rate," do you still hear the /a/ sound? What is the sound of "ae"?** *No, /ae/*

- **When you pronounce the word "taunt," do you still hear the /a/ sound? What is the sound of "au"?** *No, /au/*

- **When you pronounce the word "sank," do you still hear the /a/ sound? What is the sound of "a" in the word "sank"?** *No, /ae/*

- **When you pronounce the word "ball," do you still hear the /a/ sound? What is the sound of the word "a" in the word "ball"?** *No, /o/*

- **Why would the sound of the letter "a" change?** *The sound of the vowel is changed by the letters that come after it*

- **Do consonants change the sound of "a"? Do vowels change the sound of "a"?**
  Yes, both do

Teachers, go through the same set of questions for each of the lines of words to establish the idea that single vowel sounds are changed by both the consonants and vowels that come after the single vowel, and then summarize what has been discovered by saying:

Single vowels are called *weak* vowels because other letters, vowels and some consonants, can change the sound of the single vowel. Vowel teams are called *strong* because other consonants or vowels that come after them do not change the sound of these two letter vowels.

To aid your students in seeing the different types of vowels, you can have them sort the words in this lesson into the following categories:

Single Vowels   Vowel + E   R-controlled Vowels   Vowel Teams

Another good follow-up activity is to sort all of the vowels that your students have learned into two categories: **weak** vowels and **strong** vowels. Once students have sorted the vowels, ask questions to cement the concepts.

Vowels learned to date in this program:

- Single Vowels: "a," "e," "i," "o," "u"
- Vowel Digraphs: "oo," "au," "aw," "ai," "ay," "oa," "ow," "ea," "ey," "ee," "ae," "ie," "oe," "ue," "ar," "or," "ir," "ur," "er"
- Diphthongs: "oi," "oy," "ou," "ow"

Vowel Sort

Weak Vowels	Strong Vowels

Questions to ask:

- How many weak vowels are there? *Five, "a," "e," "i," "o," "u"*

- How many strong vowels are there? *Many, they are all of the digraphs and diphthongs*

- Why are there so many strong vowels? *Because the strong vowels are made by combining two vowels letters together*

- Do you see any patterns among the strong vowels? *All the strong vowels are two letter vowels, digraphs or diphthongs*

- What do the names "weak vowel" and "strong vowel" tell us about the letters and the sounds they make? *Weak vowels are highly influenced by other letters that come after them and their sounds change easily. The sound of strong vowels is not influenced by the letters that come after them*

- How many letters make up a weak vowel? *One*

- How many letters make up a strong vowel? *Two*

- Are there more weak vowels or more strong vowels? *There are more strong vowels and only five weak vowels: "a," "e," "i," "o," "u "*

Ask your students to create their own definitions of weak and strong vowels, then record these definitions in their spelling resource book along with examples of words for each definition.

In review sessions, have the students do this same sort several times so that you can be sure that they understand the concepts.

This might be a good time to play a Concentration game with a full deck of playing cards containing only vowel identities. When playing this game, students still match the colors or patterns on the back of the playing pieces, but before turning over each piece the student must pronounce the vowel sound and say if it is weak or strong.

The FLoSS Orthographic Pattern
Frequency - 471 words

Concepts

 How we spell the sounds /f/, /l/, /s/ and /z/ at the end of single syllable words depends upon the vowel in word. If the vowel is a digraph or diphthong, a strong two-letter vowel, these consonant sounds are spelled with the letters "f," "l," or "s," as in *life, pail,* and *base.*

If the vowel in the one syllable word is a single weak vowel, whose sound we want to retain, these sounds are spelled with "ff," "ll," or "ss," as in *puff, moss,* and *mill.*

If the vowel in the one syllable word is a single, weak vowel, followed by a consonant and then the sound /f/, /l/, or /s/, those sounds are spelled with "f," "l," or "s," as in *shelf, self,* and *half.*

Two common exceptions to this rule are "gas" and "bus"—both shortened versions of longer words, "gasoline" and "autobus". The words "gas" and "bus" should be taught by having students map the sounds onto the letters, and then memorize the letter "s" as it is the sole letter/sound that is not being spelled in an expected way.

This spelling pattern is an example of the Position Principle because we are working with sounds at the end of a one-syllable word. It is also categorized as a Protection/Position rule, because this spelling pattern is based upon whether or not the vowel needs one or two consonants to retain its sound and the consonant spellings are at the end of words.

These concepts will explain a number of different spelling patterns, including "ch-tch", "k-ck" and "ge-dge" which follow in this section of the book.

Teacher – Student Learning Dialogue

 ### Introduction

The spelling of /f/, /s/, /l/, and /z/ at the end of a one-syllable word can have two spellings: "f" or "ff," "s" or "ss," "l" or "ll" or "zz". Let's look for a pattern that will explain the differences in spellings by using the following words:

l. base   file   mile   tale   bale   knife

2. bass   fill   mill   tall   ball   puff   jazz   buzz

base = s   file = s   mile = s tale = s bale = s knife = s

bass = w   fill = w   mill=w tall = w ball= w   puff = w   jazz = w buzz = w

Using the words on line one, ask your students the following questions:

- In the word "base," how is the /s/ sound spelled? *"s"*
- What is the vowel in this word? *"ae"*
- Is that a weak or a strong vowel? *Strong*

Using the words on line two, ask your students the following questions:

- In the word "bass," how is the /s/ sound spelled? *"ss"*
- What is the vowel in this word? *"a"*
- Is that a weak or a strong vowel? *Weak*

Ask the same series of questions to help your students see the relationship between the vowels and the spelling of the final consonants.

- Do you see a pattern that would explain when /s/, /l/, /f/, or /z/ are spelled at the end of a word with one consonant letter or two? *At the end of a one-syllable word with a weak vowel, /f/ is spelled with "ff", /s/ is spelled with "ss", /l/ is spelled with "ll" and /z/ is spelled with "zz".*

  At the end of a one-syllable word that has a strong vowel, spell /f/ with "f", /s/ with "s" and /l/ with "l".

- This spelling pattern involves sounds and letters at the end of the word, so, are we using the Position Principle or the Protection Principle? *The Position Principle*
- This spelling pattern involves the weak and strong vowels and the letters that come after them in the word. Therefore, is the Protection Principle or the Position Principle working or both? *Both*

Summarize by saying:

When spelling a word that ends in the consonant "f," "l," "s" or "z" there are two ways to spell those sounds: "ff" or "f", "ll" or "l","ss" or "s" and "zz".

When the vowel in the word is a weak vowel, spell /f/, /l/, /s/ or /z/ with an "ll," "ff," "ss," or "zz".

When the vowel in the word is strong, spell the /l/, /f/, and /s/ sounds with an "l," "f" or "s."

The name of this spelling pattern is the *FLoSS* rule, which is a mnemonic that helps us remember that we are explaining the use of "f," "l" and "s" at the end of words. Another mnemonic for this rule is *Buzz Off Miss Pill*, which includes "z" in the name.

Here are some words to dictate to your students to help them practice using this pattern:

pass	loaf	feel	furl	foul	curl
chaff	less	waif	snarl	cliff	hiss
peel	off	moss	self	whirl	fill
pill	file	stiff	pool	gull	chill
half	shelf	self	snail	gloss	bliss

In a separate lesson it will be necessary to consider words such as *shelf, self,* or *half,* which appear at first glance to go against the rule of a weak vowel being paired with double consonants. However, upon further thought, it will become apparent that even though the word *shelf* has a weak vowel, it is protected by the two consonant sounds /l/ and /f/.

The "K-Ck" Orthographic Pattern
Frequency - 294 words

Concepts

 At the end of words, consonants are spelled in different ways based upon whether the vowel is weak or strong, a single vowel, a digraph or diphthong. A **weak**, single vowel needs the protection of more than one consonant letter to spell the ending /k/ sound, while a **strong** vowel does not need more than one letter to spell the ending /k/ sound.

This pattern is exactly like the FLoSS pattern, so you can expect your students to move through this lesson with ease.

Teacher – Student Learning Dialogue

 ### Introduction

At the end of a one-syllable word, there are two ways to spell /k/: "k" and "ck". Because we are dealing with a spelling that is at the end of words, this spelling pattern is based upon the Position Principle. Let's discover when to use "k" or "ck" to spell the sound of /k/ at the end of a word with this list:

back	bake
peak	peck
brick	strike
duck	duke
poke	pock

- What is the vowel in each word. Is it weak or strong? *In each pair, the vowel that is spelled with two letters is strong, and the vowel that is spelled with one letter is weak.*

Label each word with an S for a strong vowel or a W for a weak vowel:

back = W	bake = S
peak = S	peck = W
brick = W	strike = S
duck = W	duke = S
poke = S	pock = W

- How is the last sound in each word within the pairs spelled, and is it the same or different? *Sometimes the last phoneme is spelled with a single consonant "k," and sometimes it is spelled with the two consonant letters "ck".*

- How many sounds does the "ck" represent? *One*

- What would account for the different spellings of /k/ at the end of a single-syllable word. Do you see a pattern? *The words with strong vowels have "k" and the words with weak vowels have "ck".*
- If the word "back" was spelled "bak" and "ed" was added onto the end, what would happen to the weak vowel sound /a/ in that word? Would it still stay /a/ or would it change to /ae/? *It would change to /ae/ because the "e" is only one consonant letter away from the "a," and "e" can make the "a" say its letter name. The two consonant letters "ck" are needed to keep the "a" from saying /ae/.*

To summarize, when spelling a word that ends in the consonant /k/, there are two ways to spell the /k/ sound, "k" or "ck". When the vowel in the word is a weak vowel, spell the /k/ with "ck". When the vowel in the word is strong, spell the /k/ sound with "k".

Here are some words to read, spell, and sort that follow this orthographic pattern:

beak	lack	luck	stock	shook	milk
buck	look	soak	silk	deck	fork
skunk	neck	nook	weak	wake	crack
tick	stuck	seek	peak	brake	stoke

- What other spelling pattern that you have learned is this similar to? *This spelling pattern is similar to the FLoSS rule*

In a separate lesson, it will be necessary to consider words such as *silk* which appear at first glance to go against the rule of a weak vowel being paired with "k". However, upon further thought, it will become apparent that even though *silk* has a weak vowel, it is protected by two consonants, "l" and "k," and therefore does not need the "ck" to protect the weak vowel that proceeds it.

In order to focus your students' attention on the type of vowel in the word, and the letters and sounds which follow the vowel, use the sorting activity below:

Weak Vowel followed by a consonant and then /k/	**Weak Vowel** followed by /k/	**Strong Vowel** followed by /k/

The "Ch-Tch" Orthographic Pattern
Frequency – "Tch" 63 words / "Ch" not listed

Concepts

 The spelling of specific consonants at the end of a word or syllable is based upon the vowel that precedes those consonant sounds. If the vowel is **weak**, a single vowel, the final consonant sound can be spelled with "ch" or "tch," depending upon whether there is another consonant before the /ch/. If the final consonant comes directly after a **weak** vowel, with no intervening consonant, the /ch/ is spelled with "tch". If there is a **weak** vowel followed by a consonant and then /ch/, the last sound is spelled with "ch". If the vowel is **strong**, a digraph or diphthong, the final /ch/ is spelled "ch".

Teacher – Student Learning Dialogue

Introduction

At the end of a word, there are two ways to spell the /ch/ sound, "ch" and "tch". Because we are dealing with spelling of sounds at the end of a word or syllable, this is a Position Pattern. Let's discover when to use "ch," and when to use "tch".

Possible words to use to teach this rule include:

porch	patch	screech	match
peach	stitch	pooch	pitch

What is the vowel in each of the following words, and is it **weak** or **strong**? Please label the words with **weak** vowels "W" and words with **strong** vowels "S".

porch = S	patch =W	screech =S	match = W
peach = S	stitch = W	pooch =S	pitch = W

- How is the last sound in each word spelled, and is the spelling the same, or different? *Sometimes the last phoneme is spelled with "ch," and sometimes it is spelled with "tch"*

- How many sounds does the "ch" represent and how many sounds does the "tch" represent? *Both represent one sound*

- In the words that have "tch," do you pronounce the "t"? *No, we only articulate one sound, /ch/, even though there are three letters, the "t" is silent*

- In words that spell /ch/ with "ch," does a weak or strong vowel come before the /ch/? *Strong*

- In the words that spell /ch/ with "tch," what kind of vowel comes before the /ch/, weak or strong ? *Weak*

Do you see a pattern?

- Where does the common spelling pattern occur in each word, at the beginning, middle or end? *At the end*

- What is the relationship between the spelling of the ending sound and the vowel? *When the word has a strong vowel, we spell the final sound with "ch," when the word has a weak vowel, we spell the final sound with "tch"*

- This spelling pattern involves weak and strong vowels and the letters that come after the vowel in the word. Is this rule an example of the Protection Principle, the Position Principle or both? *Both*

If you were to summarize the orthographic pattern that you see in these words, what would you say? *There are two ways to spell words ending in the consonant sound /ch/. Words with a weak vowel, spell the /ch/ with a "tch". Words with a strong vowel, spell /ch/ with a "ch".*

- What other spelling pattern, that you have already learned, is this pattern similar to? *It is similar to FLoSS and the "k-ck" patterns*

In a separate lesson, you may choose to consider words such as mulch or pinch, which appear at first glance to go against the rule of a weak vowel being paired with "tch". But upon further thought, it will become apparent that even though mulch has a weak vowel, it is protected by two consonant sounds.

Much, such, which, rich and *sandwich* are also exceptions to this rule. They occur quite frequently in common texts, although they should not be presented in the first lesson.

After the pattern has stabilized in the spelling, reading, and writing of the learner, these exceptions can be memorized by creating a sentence that can then be drawn or visualized: "Which sandwich is such a rich one that I cannot eat much of it?"

Other words to work with when teaching this orthographic pattern include:

beach	bench	peach	clutch
branch	pinch	church	each
mooch	teach	hunch	reach
trench	patch	batch	catch
stitch	witch		

_____

_____

_____

_____

_____

_____

The "Ge-Dge" Orthographic Pattern

Concepts

The spelling of specific consonants at the end of a word or syllable is based upon the vowel that precedes those consonant sounds.

If a vowel is weak, a single vowel, the final consonant sound, /j/ can be spelled with "ge" or "dge" depending upon whether the vowel is weak or strong.

If the final /j/ comes directly after a weak vowel with no intervening consonant, the /j/ is spelled with "dge". If the final /j/ comes after a weak vowel plus another consonant, the /j/ is spelled with "ge".

If the vowel is strong, a digraph or diphthong, the final /j/ is spelled "ge".

Your students need to have mastered the "g" rule before learning the "ge-dge" spelling pattern.

Teacher – Student Learning Dialogue

Introduction

We are again going to investigate a Protection rule. We know from our work with the "k-ck" spelling pattern that consonant spellings at the end of a word can change based upon the type of vowel in the word. This lesson investigates the spelling of /j/ at the end of these words. Let's discover when to use "ge" or "dge" at the end of these words.

Possible words to use to teach this rule:

fudge	badge	lodge	pledge	trudge
stooge	age	huge	large	page

- **What is the vowel in each word, and is it weak or strong?** *Some words have strong vowels, others have weak vowels.*

Label each vowel as "s" for strong, or "w" for weak in those words.

fudge = W	badge = W	lodge = W	pledge = W	trudge = W
stooge =S	age = S	huge = S	large = S	page = S

- **How is the last sound in each word in this list spelled, and is it the same or different?** *Sometimes the last sound is spelled with "dge," and sometimes it is spelled with "ge".*

- **Do we pronounce the "d" letter in the words that end in "dge"?** *No, we only articulate one sound, /j/, even though there are two consonant letters for that sound in the "dge" pattern.*

- **Why do you think that "d" is there?** *To protect the weak vowel.*

- **What is the relationship between the spelling of the ending sound and the vowel?** *When the word has strong vowel, the final sound is spelled "ge,"in a word with a weak vowel, the final sound is spelled "dge".*

- **This spelling pattern involves the weak and strong vowels and the letters that come after the vowel in the word. Is this an example of the Protection Principle, the Position Principle or both?** *Both*

Please summarize the spelling pattern that you see in this list of words. When spelling a word that ends in the consonant /j/, there are two ways to spell that sound: with a weak vowel, spell the /j/ with a "dge," with a strong vowel, spell the /j/ sound with "ge".

- **What other spelling patterns that you have already learned is this similar to?** *It's similar to the FLoSS, the "ch - tch" pattern, and the "k - ck" pattern.*

In a separate lesson it will be necessary to consider words like those in the list below, which seem to go against the rule of a weak vowel being paired with "dge".

However, even though *plunge* has a weak vowel, it is protected by two consonants, "n" and "g".

range	bilge	impinge	plunge	twinge
fringe	sponge	hinge	bulge	tinge

_____

_____

_____

_____

_____

_____

_____

_____

_____

_____

_____

_____

_____

_____

_____

_____

Other Spellings at the Ends of Words: SCoRVE

This spelling/reading pattern, which occurs at the end of words involves a number of different ideas. It is remembered by the mnemonic SCoRVE because the name highlights the fact that the following sounds and letters at the end of words are unique: /s/ can be spelled with either an "-se" or a "-ce," /v/ is always spelled "-ve" at the end of words, and the /r/ can be spelled with "-re".

At the end of a word, the sound of /s/ and /z/ can be spelled several ways under what is known as the FLoSS rule, which applies to one-syllable words containing a single vowel immediately followed by the sound of /s/, /z/, /f,/ and /l/. Those sounds are spelled with the double consonants "ss," "zz," "ff," "ll".

The letter "s" can also act as a morpheme, signaling that the noun to which it is attached is plural. When "s" is added to a verb, it indicates a second person, singular verb.

The third way that the final /s/ can be spelled is "se," a spelling which helps to keep the plural "s" and the phoneme /s/ distinct.

Words like *tense* and *tens*, *freeze* and *frees*, *please* and *pleas* highlight this distinction between the plural "s" and consonant "s" or /z/ at the end of words.

Finally, the letter "c" when followed by an "e" says /s/, and this is another way to spell the sound of /s/ at the end of a word, as in *space, prance,* and *since.*

Sometimes the letter "r" is part of a vowel team, the R-controlled Vowels, but sometimes it is a consonant. At the end of words, we often see the pattern Vowel-R-E. In the words *more, core,* and *store* the vowel is an R-controlled Vowel followed by an "e". In the words *blare, scare,* and *aware*, the vowel is a Vowel + E with a consonant "r" between the Single Vowel and the "e". No matter what the job of the "r" and the "e," the pattern of Vowel-R-E is a common one, as in the words *pure, shore,* and *glare.*

In the English language, the sound of /v/ at the end of a word is always spelled "ve". Words cannot end just in a letter "v". One way of explaining this to students is to say that "v" sits on such a tiny point, it needs an "e" right next to it to hold it up.

There are so many ideas in the SCoRVE spelling pattern. It is highly recommended that you break these ideas into many separate lessons. Each lesson should begin with a review of the basic SCoRVE concept, moving to the alternate spellings for each sound/spelling pattern: for "se" portion of the SCoRVe rule, review the FLoSS rule and the plurals rule, for the "ce" portion of the SCoRVE rule, review the "c" rule, for the "re" portion of the SCoRVe rule, review the Vowel plus E and R-controlled vowels.

Here is a list of words to use to practice these ideas with your students:

goose	blaze	house	nurse	sneeze	size
prince	slice	prize	advice	snooze	twice
spice	mince	voice	truce	squeeze	doze
cure	scare	sure	fare	impure	blare
obscure	share	secure	adore	ashore	therefore
glare	snare	sleeve	evolve	revive	twelve

Spelling Cards

A number of years ago, I worked with a wonderful high school student who had made great progress in spelling and reading by learning many of the spelling patterns, then applying them efficiently in lessons.

Because it is imperative to move a student toward using independent, self-correcting strategies, he had an array of Spelling Cards containing various spelling patterns which helped him to remember them. When it was suggested that he use these cards in class, his response was "Why would I want to have all these big cards out on my desk in front of my friends? That's embarrassing! Can't you make them as small as a business card so I can carry them in my wallet, and they will be inconspicuous?" The result is on the next page, and can be copied on card stock for each of your students to use when they are correcting their written work.

When you ask a student to spell or read a list of words, place the cards that correspond with the rules you are practicing out on the table so the student can prompt herself with the ideas/spelling patterns, rather than having you repeat the ideas incessantly.

If you are having students play a game which reviews two or three of the spelling patterns, pull only those cards out of their set of Spelling Cards and display them during the game to reduce the working memory demands of the task. These cards serve as a visual reminder for students to help them retrieve and think about orthographic rules.

_____

_____

_____

_____

_____

_____

_____

_____

C Rule

If c is followed by i, e, or y,
it says /s/. If it's followed by anything
else, it says /k/.

/s/	/k/	
ci	ca	cl
ce	co	cr
cy	cu	ct

G Rule

Most of the time g says /g/.
If it's followed by i, e, or y, it
can say /j/.

/g/		/j/
ga	gl	ge
go	gr	gi
gu		gy

QU Rule

Q and U are not separable.
Qu = /kw/

Y Rule

Y_____ = /ee/
_____y_____ = /i/
_____y = /ie/
_____ _____y = /ee/
yarn
gym
my
many

—K & —CK Rule

At the end of a word, there are 2 ways
to spell /k/.
Weak, unprotected = ck
Weak, protected = k
Strong = k
back, milk, bake

—CH & —TCH Rule

At the end of a word, there are 2 ways
to spell /ch/.
Weak, unprotected = tch
Weak, protected = ch
Strong = ch
witch, trench, reach

_GE & _DGE Rule

At the end of a word, there are 2 ways
to spell /j/.
Weak, unprotected = dge
Weak, protected = ge
Strong = ge
dodge, bilge, stooge

FLoSS Rule

At the end of a 1-syllable word, if
you have a weak, unprotected vowel
followed by f, l, or s,
Double them!
puff   mill   mass

X Rule

X _____ = /z/
_____ x _____ = /ks/ or /gz/
_____x = /ks/
xylophone
exit expense fox

Part V

Reading and Spelling Long Words:
Multi-Syllable Skills

Reading and Spelling Long Words:
Multi-Syllable Skills & Concepts for the Teacher

Concept

 Many fourth, fifth and sixth grade students—and also middle school, high school, and college students—who can often read and spell shorter words, begin to falter at the multi-syllable level. As one student recently said, "If I have seen the word before and someone told me how to pronounce it, I can read it, but if I haven't been told what the word sounds like, I have no way to figure it out on my own".

By learning syllable types and morphology, your students' ability to thoughtfully read and spell multi-syllable words will greatly expand, which is why the following lessons teach syllable types while exploring prefixes, suffixes, and root syllables in words of Anglo-Saxon, Latin, and Greek origin.

These morphology lessons can add spice and meaning to our instruction, along with lessons which teach the inflectional suffixes, the past tense orthographic pattern, and the plurals orthographic pattern. The derivational suffixes, which change the part of speech of the original word—like *teach*, a verb that becomes a noun with *teacher*; and *comment*, a noun or a verb that becomes *commentator*, a person who comments—can be taught by exploring ending syllables/morphemes.

English letters, spelling patterns, syllable patterns, roots, prefixes and suffixes all come from other languages, and the four main donors—Anglo-Saxon, Latin, Greek, and French—each has its own specific syllable and affixing patterns.

Steps to Teaching Multi-Syllable Words

Reading and spelling at the multi-syllable level is very different than the one-syllable level. There are new concepts and procedures that have to be taught and practiced. These concepts and procedures will first be explained for you as a teacher and then incorporated into the lessons about syllable types and all of your lessons when students are reading and spelling multi-syllable words should include these concepts and procedures.

New vocabulary is also introduced at this level: syllable types and syllable boundaries, accented and unaccented syllables, schwa and morphemes.

Each of these concepts are explained in-depth in the following "Concept" section.

1. **Defining the structure of single and multi-syllable words**
2. **Counting syllables**
3. **Defining syllable boundaries**
4. **Steps to dividing a word into syllables**
5. **Determining accent and defining schwa**

Lessons that explicitly teach all six syllable types and syllable boundaries for each syllable type follow these sections.

Finally, each of your multi-syllable lessons should include a variety of activities to help students process and integrate the ideas. These activities are similar to the activities that were done during the one-syllable level reading and spelling lessons.

- Take an unknown word, label the vowel/consonant pattern within the word, define the category of vowel and syllable type within the word to "sound out" the word.

- Phonemic awareness exercises at the multi-syllable level

- Spelling words syllable by syllable

- Fluency activities on the multi-syllable level

- Reading connected text at the multi-syllable level

- Writing assignments with multi-syllable words

- Discussing the concept of morphemes or units of meaning in multi-syllable words

- Anglo-Saxon prefixes, suffixes and compound words, Latin roots, prefixes and suffixes and Greek combining forms

- Discussing how ending syllables in multi-syllable words signal the words grammatical category: nouns, verbs, adjectives and adverbs, as well as tense and plural markers.

- Common ending syllables are often unaccented and therefore their vowel sounds are muffled into a schwa sound.

- Etymology – exploring the history, development and meaning of words throughout time

_____

_____

_____

_____

_____

_____

_____

_____

1. Defining the Stucture of Single Syllable and Multi-Syllable Words

Concepts

 Single syllable words and multi-syllable words differ in the number of chunks that are included in the word, with each syllable having a vowel and its surrounding consonants. Some syllables only contain vowels.

In a multi-syllable word, the influence of accent patterns upon the sound of the vowel in each syllable and the meaning of the word parts, *morphemes*, are new and important concepts for students to grasp. It will be useful to explore how words are built by having your students look for patterns—rather than giving them a lecture on the structure of syllables—by beginning with the following lesson to discover the consonant and vowel patterns present in different syllables and words.

Teacher – Student Learning Dialogue

 Introduction

Here is a list of one syllable words. Let's analyze the consonant-vowel structure of these words.

a	at	my
I	us	be
met	ask	glad
dog	sky	last

Label the consonants in these words with a "c" and vowels with a "v".

<u>v</u>	<u>v</u>	<u>vc</u>	<u>vc</u>	<u>cv</u>	<u>cv</u>	<u>cvc</u>	<u>cvc</u>	<u>vcc</u>	<u>ccv</u>	<u>ccvc</u>	<u>cvcc</u>
a	I	at	us	my	be	met	dog	ask	sky	glad	last

- **What is the same in each of these words?** *They all have one and only one vowel sound.*

- **Do all of these words have consonants?** *Almost all the words have consonants before or after the vowel, a few are made up of only a vowel, some of them have consonant blends before and/or after the vowel*

Summarize what you have been discussing with your students by saying:

"Every word in English must have at least one vowel sound, They can have single consonants, consonant digraphs or consonant blends, and clusters surrounding the vowel".

"A multi-syllable word is made up of more than one of the following consonant and vowel patterns: vc, cv, cvc, cvcc, ccvc, and ccvcc. In order to read or spell a multi-syllable word, you have to learn the various syllable types and how the syllable type, as well as the accent pattern in a multi-syllable word, affect the pronunciation of the vowel and the word.

2. Counting Syllables

Concepts

 In order to read or spell a word that you don't know, you must be able to determine how many syllables are in the word and how the vowel is pronounced in each syllable. There are many ways that people determine how many syllables are in a word, but we are going to explore the most reliable method of doing this.

One way to count the number of syllables in a word is to count the number of times your jaw drops while pronouncing a word. This happens when you say a vowel sound, but this is the least efficient way to count syllables.

You can also clap the beats in a word, which are roughly equivalent to the syllables.

The most reliable way of knowing how many syllables are in a word is to identify or count how many vowel sounds it contains. There is a direct correlation between the number of syllables in a word and the number of vowel sounds it has, identifying those vowel sounds is the most reliable method of counting its syllables.

When creating lessons for counting syllables, choose an array of one-, two-, three-, four-, and five-syllable words to explore with your students. Since they may not be able to read some of the words in the lesson, say the words together, clapping each time you see a vowel within the word, pointing to the word and the vowels as you work.

An alternate presentation mode is to write the words on a piece of paper, then divide them into syllables, highlighting or labeling the vowels so students can see where the vowels appear in each syllable, along with the syllable boundaries.

Another presentation method would be to present an array of multi-syllable words, having students mark the vowel sounds before counting them.

MANY

	v		v	
m	a	n	y	

SUPERIOR

	v		v		v	v + r
s	u	p	e	r	i	o r

OVER

v	v +r
o	v e r

DIVIDEND

	v		v		v		
d	i	v	i	d	e	n	d

INDEPENDENT

v			v		v			v		
i	n	d	e	p	e	n	d	e	n	t

Additional words to work with include:

fantastic	hero	arch	assemble	establish
bear	foxes	buggy	wart	sandwich
sensible	tree	level	oval	frozen
momentary	vacancy	indestructible	mist	

Present several lessons using these concepts and strategies, then ask your students:

- **What is the most reliable method you can use to determine how many syllables are in a word?** *The number of vowel sounds tells you how many syllables are in a word*

Board Game:

Create a set of one-, two-, three-, four-, and five-syllable word cards to use with any commercial board game, and have players move across the board based on the number of syllables in the word on the card they draw from the stack.

An excellent, free resource that provides games and activities for learning orthographic patterns is the Florida Center for Reading Research (www.fcrr.org). Another useful resource for working with multi-syllable concepts is Phyllis E. Fischer's Worksheets Level 2 from Oxton Publishers, which contains many exercises for counting syllables, learning inflectional endings, syllable types, and accent patterns.

_____

_____

_____

_____

_____

_____

_____

_____

_____

_____

_____

_____

_____

_____

_____

_____

_____

3. Defining Syllable Boundaries

Concepts

 In the English language, syllables are separated in logical ways and the breaking points between syllables are called *syllable boundaries*. As there can be one and only one vowel sound in a syllable, syllable breaks occur either between two vowel sounds or between consonants and their accompanying vowels.

In words with several consonants in a row, we have to ask ourselves:

- Are these single consonants, consonant digraphs, consonant blends or consonant clusters?
- Would this combination of consonants begin a word?

These questions help to determine syllable boundaries because a consonant digraph in a word cannot be separated. In the word ashen, the syllable is broken after the digraph: *ash/en*, not *as/hen*.

If you have a consonant blend or cluster, you do not want to break the consonants into separate syllables: *a/cross*, not *ac/ross*. When there is a consonant cluster in a word, that cluster usually stays in one syllable, as in *pre/scrip/tion*, not *pres/crip/tion*.

Common consonant blends and clusters are: bl, cl, fl, gl, pl, sl, br, cr, dr, fr, gr, pr, tr, sc, sk, sm, sn, sp, st, sw, tw, scr, spl, spr, str.

Upon occasion, you do break up a series of letters that look like blends and clusters, as in *eas/tern*. We can be flexible with blends and clusters because they are made up of single consonant sounds.

In the word *eastern*, we have a root syllable *east* and a suffix *ern*, which makes the noun *east* into an adjective. If we divide this word based upon morphemes, or meaning units, the syllable boundary would come after the consonant blend "st," *east/ern*. If the syllable boundary is based upon consonant-vowel patterns, we could divide between the single consonants, *eas/tern*. The dictionary frequently lists words with a break at the morpheme boundary and according to the vowel-consonant pattern.

To help students with the pronunciation of multi-syllable words, it is useful to teach them that the majority of syllables begin with a consonant.

It is important for students to learn to be able to look at words and discern common syllable boundaries visually in order to see that longer words are made up of syllable chunks. The most common syllable boundary patterns are:

v/cv	vc/v	vc/cv	vc/ccv	v/v
o/pen	lil/y	of/ten	in/step	ne/on

After learning the basic patterns for the open and closed syllables, v/v, vc/v, vc/cv, vc/ccv, most other syllable patterns follow these basic patterns, once the vowels are identified.

vc/cv-e	vc/cvr	vc/cv (digraph)	v/cvr
in/hale	ex/port	ex/haust	spi/der

The reason for having a strategy to break an unknown word into its component syllables is to aid the reader/speller in deciphering a word they have never seen or heard. Knowing the syllable types, syllable boundaries, and accent patterns—as well as being flexible in this approach to reading or spelling a word—allows all learners to read and spell unknown words efficiently.

Most technical words in school are multi-syllable words, and these longer words are very challenging to read or spell if you do not have a strategy for deciphering them. Because these longer words are not in many students' oral vocabulary, they cannot guess the pronunciation of longer words by sounding out some of the word and using their memory of what word would fit the context of the passage they are reading.

In order to best present these ideas to students, the ideas will need to be broken up into multiple lessons which are based upon students' ages and reading abilities.

Most multi-syllable words are quite easy to read or spell if you learn syllable types and a set of steps to figure out the syllable boundaries, so we must teach each type of syllable, its vowel consonant patterns that determine the syllable boundaries, and how to play with accent patterns.

_____

_____

_____

_____

_____

_____

_____

_____

_____

_____

_____

_____

4. Steps to Dividing a Word into Syllables

Concepts

 This strategy will help students figure out what letters are the vowels in each syllable, as well as their sounds, thereby allowing them to read or spell the multi-syllable words accurately. The pronunciation of consonants is quite reliable, their sounds rarely change, while vowels are more variable based upon the syllable type and accent pattern within a word.

Imagine that you do not know how to read the word *innovation*:

1. Ask yourself if there any prefixes or suffixes that can be immediately broken off a root syllable.

The answer is *yes*, because "in" is a prefix and "tion" is a suffix, and these affixes are syllables, so we can place a diagonal line after the prefix and before the suffix to show that they are separate syllables within the word: *in/nova/tion*

2. Beginning with the first vowel in the remaining section of this word, label each vowel sound with the letter "v" until you reach the next vowel sound:

       v v
   in/nova/tion

   If you have an R-controlled Vowel, label it "vr", if you have a Vowel Plus E, label it "v+e", if you have a digraph or diphthong, only label it with a "v"—even though it is two vowel letters.

3. Label all of the consonants between the two vowel sounds:

       vcv
   in/nova/tion

4. Look for a familiar vowel consonant syllable pattern (v/v, v/cv, vc/cv, vc/v, or Consonant LE)

In the word *innovation*, the second syllable looks like an open syllable, so mark the suspected syllable boundary.

       v/cv
   in/no/va/tion

   This word has now been broken into syllables. It is made up of a prefix that is a closed syllable, two open syllables, and a suffix that is a common, irregular, ending syllable. With longer words, proceed with steps two and three until all the syllable boundaries are defined.

5. In every multi-syllable word, there is usually a pattern of accented and unaccented syllables. In an accented syllable the vowel sounds like you would expect it to, but when a syllable is unaccented, the vowel often sounds like /u/ or /i/, instead

of its regular, predictable sound. Ask yourself, "Which of the syllables might be unaccented?"

When a word ends in *-tion, -cion,* or *-sion,* the syllable that precedes it is accented. The common, irregular ending syllable in this word, *-tion,* is unaccented, its vowel has collapsed into a schwa sound, and the next to last syllable "va" is accented. There are no other syllables in this particular word that have vowels that have collapsed into a schwa, so the vowels have predictable sounds.

6. Pronounce the word.

7. Does it sound like a word you are familiar with?

8. What does it mean?

Each syllable type defines how the vowel will sound, and this is the reason we take extended time teaching students how to break words into syllables and define them as Open, Closed, R-controlled, Vowel Team, and Consonant LE syllables (*-le* preceded by a consonant in the last syllable), emphasizing the vowel sound in each syllable type.

_____

_____

_____

_____

_____

_____

_____

_____

_____

_____

_____

_____

_____

_____

5. Determining Accent and Defining Schwa

Concepts

 Another critical aspect for teaching students to correctly read and spell multi-syllable words is the creation of experiential practice that allows them to figure out how to correctly pronounce and spell vowel sounds in unaccented syllables.

When we speak our voice naturally moves up and down in volume as we stress certain syllables and words to make our messages more interesting and the information more meaningful. Sentences which have the same words, but different punctuation, are pronounced differently. The varied intonation used for questioning versus declarative or exclamatory statements is known as *prosody*.

When plainly stating an idea, a declarative statement, the voice stays pretty even throughout the sentence: "I love vanilla ice cream".

When asking a question, an interrogative statement, the voice goes up, and then down: "*I love* vanilla ice cream?"

When showing emotion or excitement, an exclamatory statement like "I love vanilla ICE CREAM!" the voice begins low and rises at the end.

Each sentence sounds a bit different because of the intent of the speaker and the punctuation marks alert the reader where to shift the voice patterns. These elements of prosody include the elongating or shortening of syllables within a single word.

Understanding and using these very abstract concepts, especially for someone with auditory discrimination problems, is often difficult. Perceiving the differences in pitch, duration, and pronunciation within a single word can be challenging. Here are some ways to teach these ideas more concretely.

Defining Accented and Unaccented Syllables

When pronouncing multi-syllable words, the volume of our voice goes up and down, and we say one or more syllables very clearly, while other syllables are spoken in a muffled tone with the vowel sounding like /u/ or /i/ instead of the its true sound.

The clearly pronounced syllables are called *accented*, while those which are slurred or have a muffled vowel are called *unaccented*.

Accented syllables are held for a longer time than unaccented syllables, which are held for a shorter duration. Accented syllables are also spoken more loudly, while unaccented syllables are pronounced more quietly.

The vowel in the accented syllable is said clearly and distinctly, while the vowel in an unaccented syllable shifts from its true sound to /u/ or /i/, and this muffled vowel is called a *schwa* vowel.

IN ACCENTED SYLLABLES:
The vowel is said clearly.
The syllable is louder.
The syllable is held for a longer duration.

IN UNACCENTED SYLLABLES:
The vowel sounds like /u/ or /i/.
The syllable is quieter.
The syllable is held for a shorter duration.

One way of making this clear to students is to represent the accented syllable with a long rectangle of paper which illustrates how that syllable is pronounced for a longer amount of time and a shorter piece of paper that represents the unaccented syllable which is pronounced for a shorter amount of time.

ACCENTED	UNACCENTED

Have students raise the accented syllable higher than the unaccented syllable to show how their voice is louder when pronouncing accented syllables and quieter when pronouncing unaccented syllables.

Make a stickie note with the vowel sounds /u/ and /i/ on it, then ask students to place that stickie note on the unaccented syllable to show that the vowel in that syllable is saying /u/ or /i/ rather its expected sound.

/u/ /i/

Almost every multisyllable word has a pattern of accented and unaccented syllables, and the pronunciation of the vowels will be determined by this accent pattern. Be careful though, because sometimes in a two-syllable word neither syllable will be unaccented.

Here is a list of words in which the first syllable is accented:

bot´tom	tick´et
hic´cup	satch´el
jack´et	blank´et
mol´lusk	fun´nel

Here is a list of words in which the second syllable is accented:

at tack´	pro duce´
pos sess´	af fect´
re bel´	com press´

Use the different sized pieces of paper to demonstrate the pattern of accented and unaccented syllables in each of these words.

One of the best resources for lists of words with accented and unaccented syllables is *Concept Phonics Worksheets* by Phyllis E. Fischer, Ph.D. published by Oxton House Publishers in Farmington, Maine.

In order to prove how important accent is to meaning, you can use words whose meaning and part of speech changes based upon which syllable is accented and which is unaccented:

reb´ el (noun)	re bel´ (verb)
pro´ duce (noun)	pro duce´ (verb)
con´ tent (noun)	con tent´ (adjective)
con´ duct (noun)	con duct´ (verb)

With so many ideas about accented and unaccented syllables, and even more about which syllable is accented in a three-, four-, or five-syllable word, it is important to present only one or two ideas at a time so you don't overwhelm your students.

A useful resource for learning and practicing accent patterns in two-, three-, and four-syllable words is *Megawords 3* by Kristin Johnson & Polly Bayrd (2004).

In spelling, strategies have to be developed to aid the speller in sorting out which vowel, "a," "e," "i," "o," "u," or "y" has shifted to the schwa sound. Learning about morpheme families, words that have common roots, can help with this process.

An example of a morpheme family would be:

colony	colonial	colonize	colonist

The syllable boundaries and accent patterns shift from word to word in this morpheme family because each word has a different number of syllables, yet they all have the same root syllable. Knowing the different words in a morpheme family can help the speller solve the mystery of which vowel letter is spelling the schwa sound. As the number of syllables is added or subtracted from the root, the accent pattern shifts. As the accent shifts, the vowel letters revert to their original sound.

In the word *colony*, the second syllable is unaccented, and the vowel in that syllable sounds like /u/.

In the word *colonial*, the second syllable is accented, and the vowel is clearly heard, with the /oe/ telling the speller that the /u/ in the second syllable of the word *colony* is spelled with an "o".

These ideas move between the domains of vocabulary, morphology, and spelling. This type of lesson must be scaffolded carefully with younger students and those with weak vocabulary skills.

To circumvent this problem, teach the meanings of the words within the morpheme family, the grammatical function of each by using the words in sentences, as well as how the shifting accent patterns give hints about how to spell and pronounce the words.

In each of the lessons that teach syllable types, words will be included to practice these ideas of accented and unaccented syllables.

Open and Closed Syllable Lesson

Concepts

Before beginning lessons about syllable types, students must understand the following concepts, be able to demonstrate their knowledge, and explain the concepts:

- What is a syllable? (Explained in the *Defining Attributes of Single and Multisyllable Words* section)

- How can you determine how many syllables are in a word? (Explained in the *Counting Syllables* section)

- What are accented and unaccented syllables, and how does the presence or absence of accent in a syllable affect the vowel sound? (Explained in the *Accent* section)

There are different types of syllables, and each syllable type is categorized based upon the type of vowel it contains.

The metaphor of an old-fashioned train is a meaningful way for illustrating how words that are made up of more than one-syllable are built.

Teacher – Student Learning Dialogue

Introduction

Multi-syllable words and old-fashioned trains have a lot of common characteristics. Multi-syllable words can be made up of two, three, four, or more different syllables, just as trains can have a varying number of cars.

Just like trains that have unique cars at the front called *locomotives*, words can have specific syllables in the initial part of the word called *prefixes*, which are added to words to change their meaning:

dress – <u>un</u>dress

view – <u>pre</u>view

like – <u>dis</u>like

Trains also have a special car at the end called a *caboose*, and many multisyllable words have a special category of syllables that always come at the end of the word called *suffixes* which are added to words to tell us what their job is in a sentence:

- Is this word a noun, an adjective, a verb or an adverb?

- If the word is a noun, is it naming one or many things, is it singular or plural?

- If the word is a verb, is the action described by the verb happening now or in the past?

Trains can have any number of different types of cars between the locomotive and the caboose: open cars, closed cars, cattle cars, passenger cars. Multi-syllable words can have different types of syllables:

Open Syllables	R-controlled Syllables
Closed Syllables	Vowel Team Syllables
Vowel plus E Syllables	Consonant LE Syllables

There is also a group of syllables at the end of some words called Common Irregular Ending Syllables.

Learning about all of these types of syllables will make reading and spelling longer words much easier.

In this lesson, we will learn about two syllable types by exploring the vowel and consonant patterns within each syllable as we figure out how the vowel sounds in each type.

me	I	so	a
met	it	sop	at

- What kind of vowel do we have in each of these words, a single vowel or a vowel digraph? *A single vowel*

- Does the vowel sound the same in each word? *No*

There has to be a reason for the difference in the sound of the vowel. Let's look at where the vowel is in the following words—at the beginning, middle or end of the word—and whether the last letter in each word is a vowel or a consonant.

Mark the last letter in each word with either a "v" for vowel or a "c" for consonant.

me = V	met = C
I = V	it = C
so = V	sop = C
a = V	at = C

- When the single vowel is at the end of the word, does it say its letter name or its sound on the Single Vowel Staircase (the short sound)? *It says its letter name*

- When the single vowel is at the beginning or the middle of the word, followed by a consonant, does it say its letter name or its Single Vowel Staircase sound? *It says its Single Vowel Staircase sound*

Defining Open and Closed Syllables

When a syllable has a single vowel at the end of a word or syllable *followed by nothing*, that syllable is called an *open syllable*, and that single vowel says its letter name.

When we learned about consonants and vowels, vowels were labeled *open phonemes* because we put our jaw, tongue, and lips in a certain position and pass air through that structure. Since this syllable ends in a vowel, we label the syllable an *open syllable.*

When a syllable has a single vowel followed by one or more consonants in a syllable or word, it is a *closed syllable,* and that single vowel says its Single Vowel Staircase sound.

When we learned about the consonants, we labeled them *closed phonemes* because we use some part of our mouth to close off the air. A syllable that ends with a consonant is labeled a *closed syllable.*

Students should be able to state these syllable definitions. Have them write the definitions in their rulebooks, giving examples of each syllable type. In the next lesson, you will explore multi-syllable words that are made up of open and closed syllables, and including these in the lesson, as well as the diacritical marks for each syllable type is very important.

Here is a possible definition for an open syllable: a syllable containing a single vowel with no letters following the vowel that says its letter name: *i/ris, o/pen, hi, and I.*

Here is a possible definition of a closed syllable: a syllable that has a single vowel followed by one or more consonants that says its sound on the Single Vowel Staircase: *cov/er, ban/ dit,* and *hit.*

Schwa

When we pronounce multi-syllable words, the volume of our voice goes up and down as we say one syllable very clearly, with other syllables having a muffled tone, making the vowel sound like /u/ or /i/ instead of the vowel's true sound.

We also say one syllable for a longer time, and other syllables for a shorter duration. The syllable with the clearly spoken vowel is an accented syllable, while the syllable in which we muffle the vowel is an unaccented syllable. When the vowel shifts from its true sound to /u/ or /i/, that vowel sound has been muffled into a schwa.

Accented Syllables

Say the vowel clearly.

Say the syllable more loudly.

Say the syllable for a longer duration.

Unaccented Syllables

Vowel sounds like /u/ or /i/.

Say the syllable quietly.

Say the syllable for a shorter duration.

Sometimes humming a word can help you to better hear its accent pattern, but be careful, sometimes *neither* syllable in a multi-syllable word will be unaccented.

Words to practice determining which syllables are accented or unaccented, and which syllable has a vowel that has muffled into a schwa sound include:

First Syllable Accented	Second Syllable Accented
cactus	unless
problem	confess
bottom	connect
blossom	attack
gallon	affect
pollen	collect

Have students represent the accented and unaccented syllables with pieces of paper as described previously.

_____

_____

_____

_____

_____

_____

_____

_____

_____

_____

_____

_____

_____

_____

_____

_____

_____

_____

_____

Vowel Consonant Patterns for Open Syllables: V/CV, V/V

Concepts

After teaching the open syllable type, it is helpful to explore vowel-consonant patterns for open syllables. Instead of telling the information to your students, engage them in exploring words and discovering the patterns. Here is a sample lesson for open syllables.

Teacher – Student Learning Dialogue

Introduction

Here is a list of real words that contain some open syllables and some closed syllables. We will be looking for particular vowel consonant patterns in the open syllables.

open	even	neon	
iris	boa	level	lily

Beginning with the first vowel in each word, mark vowels with the letter V and each consonant between the vowels with the letter C.

vcv	vcv	vv	vcv	vv	vcv	vcv
open	even	neon	iris	boa	level	lily

V	C	V	
o	p	e	n

V	C	V	
e	v	e	n

V	V	
n	e	o	n

V	C	V	
i	r	i	s

V	V	
b	o	a

V	C	V	
l	e	v	e	l

V	C	V	
l	i	l	y

What patterns of vowels and consonants did you find in these words? *VCV and VV*

In the English language, there can be one and only one vowel sound per syllable. Therefore, with the VV pattern, we have to break the word into syllables between these two vowel sounds (V/V): ne/on, bo/a.

With the pattern VCV, there are two possible ways to break the syllables, *before* the consonant or *after* the consonant.

The most common way to break up this pattern is to make the syllable boundary after the first vowel, thus creating an open syllable pattern (V/CV): *o/pen, si/lent.*

If you make the syllable boundary after the consonant, you create a closed syllable, and the vowel will say its sound on the Single Vowel Staircase. *lev/el   lil/y*

Try both patterns, pronounce the word, and see which results in a real word. In the words *open* and *silent,* the syllable boundary is after the first vowel. Once you make the first syllable break in each of these words, you have to determine if the second syllable is an open syllable or a closed syllable so you will know how to pronounce the vowel in the second syllable.

Determining accent in a word also helps to decide how to pronounce the vowels. In an accented syllable, the vowel says its expected sound. The vowel in the unaccented syllable is muffled, and sounds like /u/ or /i/.

To test which syllable is accented, play with the vowel sound like this:

1. Say the vowel as a regular vowel.
2. Change that vowel sound to say /u/ or /i/.
3. Listen to the words and ask yourself which pronunciation sounds like a real word.

If the vowel sound says /u/ or /i/, the syllable is unaccented. If the vowel sound says its expected sound, the syllable is accented.

In an open syllable, the vowel says its letter name unless the syllable is unaccented. Let's apply these ideas to some of the words in this lesson.

In the word neon we would separate the syllables between the two vowels.

v/v

ne/on

- What type of syllable is the first syllable? *Open*
- How would you pronounce the first syllable? */nee/*
- What type of syllable is the second syllable? *It is a closed syllable because it has a single vowel followed by a consonant*
- What is the sound of the vowel in a closed syllable? *It says its Single Vowel Staircase sound*

Both syllables are saying their expected sound, so neither syllable is unaccented.

- What do you think this word sounds like? Does it sound like a familiar word, and what does it mean?

ne/on

Let's examine the word "boa," which has two vowel sounds next to each other. Is this a one-syllable or a two-syllable word?

vv

boa

Sometimes "oa" is a digraph (Two Vowel Friends). In this word, "oa" is acting as two single vowels, and because every syllable in a word can have one and only one vowel sound, it is a two-syllable word.

145

- Is the first syllable open or closed? *Open*
- What does a vowel sound like in an open syllable? *It says its letter name*
- Is the second syllable open or closed? *Open*

The vowel in the first syllable in the word "boa" is saying its expected sound in an open syllable, /oe/. The second syllable is unaccented, so the vowel sounds like /u/, a schwa.

- When you read the word, does it sound familiar to you and what does it mean?

The word IRIS
Mark the vowels with the letter V and the consonants between the vowels with a C.

- If we break the syllables apart after the first vowel, the first syllable will be an open syllable. What does a single vowel sound like in an open syllable? *It says its letter name*
- If we break the syllables apart after the first consonant, the first syllable will be an R-controlled syllable. What does a single vowel sound like in an R-controlled syllable? *If "ir" is an R-controlled Vowel that says /r/*
- The second syllable in this word is closed. How would the word sound if the first syllable is open? *i/ris* Closed? *ir/is*
- Which pronunciation sounds like a word you know? *i/ris*

The word LEVEL
Mark the vowels with the letter V and the consonants between the vowels with a C.

- If we break the syllables apart after the first vowel, the first syllable will be an open syllable. What does a single vowel sound like in an open syllable? *It says its letter name, so "le" will say /lee/*
- If we break the syllables apart after the first consonant, the first syllable will be a closed syllable. What does a single vowel sound like in a closed syllable? *It says its sound on the Single Vowel Staircase, so if the first syllable in this word is closed it would say /lev/*
- The second syllable in this word is unaccented, so the second "e" sounds like /u/. Is this word pronounced /lee vul/ or /lev ul/? */lev ul/*
- What are the two-vowel consonant patterns that we have discovered for open syllables in this experiment? *V/CV and V/V*

After teaching these concepts have your students practice breaking words into syllables, and reading and spelling words with the patterns they have learned.

Developing flexibility with the pronunciation of vowels is a critical skill for reading and spelling words, and practicing being flexible with syllable boundaries and accent patterns should be an essential component of any multi-syllable lesson.

Vowel Consonant Patterns for Closed Syllables: VC/V, VC/CV

Concepts

After teaching the open syllable type, it is helpful to explore the various vowel consonant patterns for the closed syllable type. Be sure to engage your students in a dialogue to explore words and discover their patterns, rather than just giving them the information. Here is a sample lesson for closed syllables.

Teacher – Student Learning Dialogue

Introduction

Here is a list of real words that contain only closed syllables that we will use to look for the particular vowel consonant patterns in closed syllables.

metal   happen   within   until

The word METAL

We are going to divide these words into syllables, and every syllable can have *only one vowel.*

Mark the vowels with the letter V and the consonants between the vowels with a C.

- If we break the syllables apart after the first vowel, the first syllable will be an open syllable.
- What does a single vowel sound like in an open syllable? *It says its letter name*
- If we break the syllables apart after the first consonant, the first syllable will be closed. What does a single vowel sound like in a closed syllable? *The Staircase Sound*
- The second syllable in this word is unaccented, so the vowel is muffled into a schwa and says /u/. Which sounds like a word you know, me/tal or met/al? *met/al*
- What was the vowel consonant pattern for the closed syllable in the word "metal"? *VC/V*

The word HAPPEN

Mark the vowels with the letter V and the consonants between the vowels with a C.

- When you see two of the same consonants in a row within a word, twin consonants, divide the syllables between the two consonants. *Hap/pen*
- Both of these syllables in this word are closed syllables because they have a single vowel and end in a consonant. Can you pronounce this word? *Happen*
- What was the vowel consonant pattern for the closed syllable in the word "happen"? *VC/CV*

- When two of the same consonants sit side by side between two vowel sounds as in the word "happen," they are called twin consonants because they are the same letter and the syllable break is between these two letters. *Hap pen*

The word WITHIN
Mark the vowels with the letter V and the consonants between the vowels with a C. Mark the "th" with one C because it is consonant digraph, two letters making one sound.

- If we break the syllables apart after the first vowel, the first syllable will be an open syllable. What does a single vowel sound like in an open syllable? *It says its letter name*
- If we break the syllables apart after the first consonant, the first syllable will be a closed syllable. What does a single vowel sound like in a closed syllable? *The Staircase Sound*
- In this word the first and second syllables are closed, and the vowels say their Staircase Sound. Can you pronounce this word, and does it sound like a word you recognize? *With in*
- What was the vowel consonant pattern for the closed syllable in the word, within? *VC/V*

The word UNTIL
Mark the vowels with the letter V and the consonants between the vowels with a C.

- When you see two different consonants in a row within a word, divide the syllables between the two consonants.
- The first syllable and second syllable in this word are closed syllables because they both have a single vowel and each syllable ends in a consonant.
- What will the vowels in each of these syllables say? */u/, /i/*
- Can you pronounce the word? *un til*
- What was the vowel consonant pattern for the closed syllable in the word "until"? *VC/CV*
- What are the two vowel consonant patterns that we have discovered for closed syllables in this lesson? *VC/V, VC/CV*

As you teach the various vowel-consonant patterns, it will be helpful to have your students visually recognize the patterns. One way of doing this is to create a set of flashcards with the patterns v/v, v/cv, vc/v, vc/cv, and ask your students to identify the closed or open syllable pattern in each word.

After this, have the students divide the words into syllables, even cutting the syllables apart and sorting them based on the VC pattern. Some of the following words contain the consonant blends "-nd," "-sk," and "str-," which are not usually separated.

Words to work with include:

sudden	muffin	attic	traffic	gossip	tuba
himself	coffin	catnip	global	happen	bandbox
inland	pilot	sunfish	within	muskrat	publish
cactus	infect	petal	kidnap	bandage	ostrich

Students like to write words on cards and cut the syllables apart. These cards can then be used for making up words by putting two- or three-syllables together.

Have your students practice determining where the accented syllable is by giving each of them a set of different sized cards to illustrate which syllable is accented and which syllable is unaccented in the following words (see page 138).

The first list below has words in which the first syllable is accented, and the second list has words with the second syllable accented. Work with only one section at a time, and once your students have mastered identifying accent in the first or second syllable, make up a list that contains both types of syllables.

First Syllable Accented

bottom	sudden	mammal
puppet	gallon	cannon
kennel	pilot	vocal
flannel	bacon	global

Second Syllable Accented

adjust	cement	sedan
connect	baton	canal
consult	admit	adult

_____

_____

_____

_____

_____

_____

_____

_____

Vowel plus E Syllable Lesson

Teacher – Student Learning Dialogue

 ### Introduction

There are six different syllable types. We have learned two of them, open and closed syllables. In this lesson, we will discover a new syllable type, the Vowel plus E syllable.

In the following list of words, pay attention to the vowels in each syllable. Identify whether the syllable has a single vowel, indicating that the syllable is either open or closed or if the vowel in the syllable is a Vowel plus E.

promote	extreme	provide
became	inside	canine

What are the vowels in the word "promote"?

		v		v + e		
p	r	o	m	o	t	e

This is a two-syllable word.

- What type of vowel is the first syllable in this word, a single vowel or a digraph? *Single vowel*
- What type of vowel is the second vowel, a single vowel or Vowel plus E? *Vowel plus E, it is a vowel digraph*

Let's divide this word into syllables so we will know whether to pronounce the first syllable as an open syllable or as a closed syllable. You have marked the vowels, please mark the consonants between them.

		v	c	v + e		
p	r	o	m	o	t	e

This word has a VCV pattern. The first syllable could be an open V/CV pattern or a closed VC/V pattern. Try to pronounce the word both ways. Which pronunciation sounds like a real word?

pro/mote   prom/ote

The first syllable is an open syllable, and the second syllable is a Vowel plus E syllable.

Let's look at the other words in this lesson.

v	c c	c	c	v + e	
e	x	t	r	e m	e

The letter "x" represents two consonant sounds, and the letters "tr" are a consonant blend. When dividing words into syllables, we usually do not divide up a consonant blend, so this word will be divided after the "x".

ex/treme

- **Is the first syllable open or closed?** *Closed*
- **How does the single vowel sound in a closed syllable sound, /e/ or /ee/?** */e/*
- **What is the vowel in the second syllable, a single vowel or Vowel plus E?** *Vowel plus E*

The vowel in the second syllable is a Vowel plus E, so it is a Vowel plus E syllable. Can you pronounce this word? Does it sound like a word you recognize?

Proceed through the rest of the words in this lesson, using the same instructions and questions. After going through all the words, share the following definition for a Vowel plus E syllable with students, and have them add it to their rulebooks:

When a single vowel in a syllable is followed by one consonant and then an "e," that vowel says its letter name and the syllable is labeled a Vowel plus E syllable. This is another pattern which enables the vowel to say its letter name.

- **What other syllable pattern results in a vowel saying its letter name?** *An open syllable*

Vowel Consonant Patterns for Vowel plus E Syllables

V/CCV+E, VC/C+E, VC/CCV+E

Concepts

After teaching the Vowel plus E syllable lesson, work with words that follow the vowel consonant pattern for this syllable type. The basic patterns for the open and closed syllables V/CV, VC/V, VC/CV, and VC/CCV are the template that most other syllable patterns follow.

Because these syllable patterns are taught in a progressive order, you can incorporate the concepts from previous lessons. The words in this lesson will incorporate open and closed syllable types to help students review.

Teacher – Student Learning Dialogue

Introduction

The basic syllable boundary patterns we have learned so far are V/V, V/CV, VC/V, VC/CV and VC/CCV.

There can be single consonants in each of these patterns or consonant digraphs.

We can also have consonant blends that we want to keep in the same syllable, VCC/CV and VC/CCV.

The vowels in these patterns can be single vowels or Vowels Plus E.

Here is a list of real words that contain Vowel plus E syllables. We are going to look for the particular vowel consonant patterns for these syllables.

impose	feline	migrate
inhale	sunrise	include

Beginning with the first vowel in each word, mark the vowels with the letter V and the consonants between them with the letter C. When you have a Vowel plus E, mark the vowel letter with V+E.

v	c	c	v + e	
i	m	p	o	s	e

v	c	v +e	
f	e	l	i	n	e

v	c	c	v+e	
m	i	g	r	a	t	e

v	c	c	v+e	
i	n	h	a	l	e

v	c	c	v + e	
s	u	n	r	i	s	e

v	c	c	c	v + e	
i	n	c	l	u	d	e

- In each word, how many vowel letters are there? *Three*
- How many vowel sounds are there? *Two*
- What type of vowels are in these words, single vowels and/or digraphs? *Both*

In the English language there can be one and only one vowel sound in each syllable. What is the vowel consonant pattern in the word "impose"?

v	c	c	v + e	
i	m	p	o	s	e

Let's figure out the syllable boundary in this word. The VC/CV+E is similar to the closed pattern, VC/CV, and the syllables are divided between the two consonants in the middle of the word.

- What type of syllable is the first syllable in "impose," open, closed or Vowel plus E? *Closed*

- What is the vowel in the second syllable? What type of syllable is it? *Vowel plus E*

We can now see that the syllable boundary splits between the consonants, VC/CV+E.

- What is the vowel consonant pattern in the word "feline"?

	v	c	v + e	
f	e	l	i	n	e

The V/CV+E is similar to the open pattern V/CV, and the syllables are divided between the first vowel and the first consonant in the middle of the word.

- What type of syllable is the first syllable in the word "feline," open, closed or Vowel plus E? *Open*

- What is the vowel in the second syllable? What type of syllable is it? *Vowel Plus E*

The syllable boundary splits between the consonants V/CV+E.

Work through all of the words in this lesson using the same set of questions and procedures.

The following list of words can be used to practice determining which syllable is accented and which is unaccented. Be sure to talk about the change in the vowel sound in the unaccented syllables, as in the words *practice, office* and *message*. The sound of the vowel in the second syllables of these words is muffled into schwa. Also, ask the students about the multiple jobs of the letter "e" at the end of some of these words. In the word *practice*, the "e" is making the "c" say /s/, and in the word *message*, the "e" is influencing the "g" to say /j/.

practice	mistake	reptile	cabbage	suppose
office	message	confuse	combine	stampede
collide	assume	trombone	cascade	captive

Vowel Team Syllable Lesson

Concepts

Vowel team syllables have two letter vowels, digraphs, and diphthongs. The basic patterns for the open and closed syllables V/V, V/CV, VC/V, VC/CV, and VC/CCV are the same patterns for vowel team syllable boundaries. When labeling the vowels in this lesson, have your students mark each digraph or diphthong with only one letter V, because these vowels represent only one sound.

Teacher – Student Learning Dialogue

Introduction

There are six different syllable types. We have learned about open, closed and Vowel plus E syllables. Let's see how this new syllable type is unique with this list of words:

devour	doomsday	stairway	withdraw	rainbow
mislead	cookbook	railroad	steamboat	blackmail

Underline or circle the vowels in each of these words. *"e," "ou," "oo," "ay," "ai," "i," "aw," "ow," "ea," "oa," "a"*

- What category of vowels do these spellings represent? Single vowels or vowel teams? *Both*
- How many syllables are in each word? *Two, because each word has two vowel sounds*

When a syllable has a vowel team for a vowel, we call that syllable a vowel team syllable. Mark the vowels and the consonants between the vowels in each word to divide the words into syllables. Remember, vowel teams only are marked with one V, and consonant digraphs are only marked with one C. When we divide syllables, we do not break apart consonant digraphs or vowel teams.

devour

Where shall we break up the syllables in this word? Mark the vowels in this word with a V and the consonants between the vowels with a C.

vcv

devour

When you see the VCV pattern, it can be divided after the first vowel creating an open syllable V/CV or after the consonant VC/V creating a closed syllable.

- The most common way to separate syllables with this pattern is the open pattern. If the first syllable is an open syllable, how will you pronounce the vowel, /e/ or /ee/? */ee/*

- In the word "devour," what type of syllable is the first syllable? Open, closed or Vowel plus E? *Open*
- In the word "devour," what type of syllable is the second syllable? *A vowel team syllable*
- What is the vowel in the second syllable? *"ou"*
- How does that vowel sound? */ou/*
- Can you now read this two-syllable word? *Devour*

Continue through the rest of the words in this lesson and ask the same set of questions. The correct syllable boundaries are listed below:

de/vour	dooms/day	stair/way	with/draw	rain/bow
mis/lead	cook/book	rail/road	steam/boat	black/mail

_____

_____

_____

_____

_____

_____

_____

_____

_____

_____

_____

_____

_____

_____

_____

_____

_____

Vowel Consonant Patterns for Vowel Team Syllables

VC/V, V/CV, V/V, VC/CV

Teacher – Student Learning Dialogue

Introduction

Let's look at the vowel consonant patterns in these words and see if there are any new patterns that tell us where to break apart the syllables.

v c v	v c c v	v c v	v c c v
pronoun	compound	thousand	yellow

These are the same patterns that we used when dividing open, closed and Vowel plus E syllables.

What is the vowel in each syllable? What type of syllable is in each word? How is the vowel pronounced?

V / C	**VC / CV**	**V / CV**	**VC / CV**
pro/ noun	com / pound	thou / sand	yel / low
Open, Vowel Team	Closed, Vowel Team	Vowel Team, Closed	Closed, Vowel Team
/oe/ /ou/	/o/ /ou/	/ou/ /a/	/e/ /oe/

In all of our previous lessons we have considered accent, and how accent affects the sound of the vowel in an unaccented syllable. A two-syllable word can have a primary accent on the first or the second syllable or there can be no primary accent in a two-syllable word.

Let's decide what the accent patterns are in the following words. Remember, a good test for whether a syllable is unaccented is if the vowel sound in a syllable says /u/ or /i/ instead of its expected sound, the schwa sound. An unaccented syllable doesn't always have a schwa sound.

Ask yourself, "Which syllable am I saying longer? Louder? More clearly?" That syllable will be the accented syllable. Use an acute diacritical mark to show the accented syllable.

pro/noun	ex/ploit	thou/sand	aim/less	be/low
ca/boose	com/pound	yel/low	de/tain	sail/boat

pro'/noun	ex/ploit'	thou'/sand	aim'/less	be/low'
ca/boose'	com'/pound	yel'/low	de/tain'	sail'/boat

R-controlled Vowel Syllable Lesson

Teacher – Student Learning Dialogue

 ### Introduction

There are six different syllable types, this is the fifth. The name or category of each syllable type is based upon the vowel sound within that syllable. Words that have single vowels can be open or closed, words with Vowel plus E are Vowel plus E syllables, and syllables that have vowel digraphs or diphthongs are vowel team syllables. In this lesson, we will learn a new syllable type that is based on its vowel.

Since your students are now quite familiar with the concepts of differentiating syllable types, you might have the words in this lesson randomly written on the board or an overhead for them to copy and conduct an open sort.

After all the students have finished their sorts, proceed using the questions in the lesson. You can also ask students to share what they have discovered with a partner, after which they can share their ideas with the whole group. Such response requirements help to keep all students actively engaged in thinking.

Possible words to use to teach this syllable type include:

charcoal	better	roadster	ardent	farmer	border	cancer
murmur	burlap	pointer	scorcher	disturb	firmest	stormy

- **What letters represent the vowels in each syllable?** *"ar," "oa," "e," "er," "or," "a," "ur," "oi," "ir," "y"*

  Label each vowel:

  SV = Single vowel

  VT = Vowel team

  VR = R-controlled vowel

- What R-controlled vowels are in each word? *"ir," "ur," "er," "ar," "or"*

When a single vowel in a syllable is followed by an "r", the syllable is labeled an R-controlled syllable because the "r" changes the sound of the vowel that precedes it. "Ir," "ur," and "er" all say the same sound, /r/. "Ar" and "or" have distinct sounds.

Vowel Consonant Patterns for R-controlled Syllables

VC/CVr, V/CVr, Vr/CVr, VrC/CV

Concepts

The R-controlled syllable boundaries follow the basic patterns of V/V, V/CV, VC/V, and VC/CV. The vowel in an R-controlled syllable should be labeled VR.

Teacher – Student Learning Dialogue

Introduction

Here is a list of words that contain R-controlled syllables. Let's figure out the syllable boundaries for this type of syllable.

barber	mother	corner	hurtful	girder

- When a vowel is immediately followed by the letter "r," that "r" functions as a marker. What is the job of the "r" in the words on the board? *The "r" changes the sound of the vowel that comes before it*

Beginning with the first vowel in each word, mark the vowels with the letter V and the consonants between the vowels with the letter C. Mark all of the R-controlled vowels VR, mark the consonant digraphs with only one C.

	v r		c		vr	
b	a	r	b	e	r	

	v		c		vr	
m	o	t	h	e	r	

	v r		c		vr	
c	o	r	n	e	r	

	v r		c	c	v	
h	u	r	t	f	u	l

	v r		c		v r	
g	i	r	d	e	r	

To divide these words into syllables, it is helpful to begin with the ending syllable that have R-controlled vowels. Syllables like to start with a consonant, so look for the syllable breaks to be between the first syllable and the CVr.

vr /cvr	v / cvr	vr / cvr	vrc / cv	vr /cvr
bar/ber	mo/ther	cor/ ner	hurt/ful	gir/der

If you think of the "VR" part of the consonant vowel pattern as only a vowel, you will see the familiar syllable boundary patterns of V/CV, VC/V, VC/CV, VC/CCV.

When a syllable has a single vowel followed by an "r," it is labeled as an R-controlled syllable. The R is such a powerful letter that it affects the pronunciation of the single vowel that comes before it.

Say the following words and see if the R-controlled syllables say the sound that you would expect. Is the other syllable in the word accented or unaccented? Does either syllable collapse into a schwa?

ci/der	des/ert	a/larm	a/corn
pa/per	clev/er	shiv/er	wa/ger

ci´/der	des´/ert	a/larm´	a´/corn
pa´/per	clev´/er	shiv´/er	wa´/ger

The only schwa syllable in this list of words is the first syllable in the word "alarm".

_____

_____

_____

_____

_____

_____

_____

_____

_____

_____

_____

_____

_____

_____

_____

_____

_____

_____

Consonant LE Syllable Lesson

Teacher – Student Learning Dialogue

Introduction

The last syllable type that we are going to learn is a bit different than the other syllable types because of its vowel and the fact that this syllable only appears as a final syllable. Let's find out about its vowel sound using the following words.

maple	ma/ple
rifle	ri/fle
struggle	strug/gle
topple	top/ple
tremble	trem/ble

These words have been divided into syllables. Identify the first syllable, is it open or closed?

maple	ma = open
rifle	ri = open
struggle	strug = closed
topple	top = closed
tremble	trem = closed

- Looking at the second syllables, what is visually the same about these syllables? *They all have a consonant followed by "le"*

Pronounce these ending syllables and have the students repeat them in order to correctly answer the next question.

- How many sounds are in these ending syllables, two or three? *Two*
- What letters represent those sounds? *A consonant and the letters "le"*
- Every syllable must have a vowel. What is the vowel in these ending syllables? *"e"*
- Is the "e" making the /e/ sound or is it silent? *It is silent*

The reason that there is an "e" in each of these syllables is that every syllable must have a vowel. Even though the "e" in these syllables is silent, it acts as a marker to alert us that this is a syllable. If there is any vowel sound at all, we could argue that there is a quickly pronounced schwa sound between the consonant and the "l".

- Where do these syllables occur in each word, at the beginning or the end of the words? *The end*

When you see an ending syllable that follows the pattern, a consonant followed by an "le," this syllable is labeled a consonant LE syllable, and the letter "e" in that syllable is silent.

Have students add this definition to their rulebook.

Vowel Consonant Pattern for Consonant LE Syllables: /CLE

Concepts

Because all of these syllable patterns have been taught in a progressive order, you can incorporate all the syllable types from previous lessons into this lesson. A student should have been taught and worked with open, closed, Vowel plus E, vowel team and R-controlled syllable patterns before exploring the consonant LE pattern. The words in this lesson will incorporate those syllable types to help the student review these other syllable types.

Teacher – Student Learning Dialogue

Introduction

Here is a list of real words that contain consonant LE syllables. We are going to look for the particular vowel-consonant patterns to determine the syllable boundaries.

bundle	trouble	mettle	stumble	stable

- **How many syllables in each of these words?** *Two*
- **How do you know that?** *Each syllable can have one and only one vowel sound and each of these words have two vowel sounds*
- **What is the same about all of these words?** *They all end with a consonant followed by an "l" and an "e"*
- **Where does this syllable pattern occur, in the beginning or the ending syllable?** *The ending syllable*

When you see an LE preceded by a consonant in the last syllable in a word, that syllable is labeled as a consonant LE syllable. To break this syllable off from the rest of the word, begin with the "e" at the end of the word, label it with the number 1. Count backwards, labeling the "l" that precedes the "e" with the number 2 and the consonant that precedes the "l" with the number 3. The syllable boundary for a consonant LE syllable is before that third letter.

321	321	321	321
sta/ble	met/tle	trou/ble	bun/dle

Words for your students to read and spell with consonant LE:

babble	cable	grumble	marble	bible	crumble
fable	sable	bauble	dribble	gobble	humble
rumble	bubble	enable	bugle	simple	candle
temple	wiggle	little	rattle	jungle	middle
giggle	fiddle	whittle	bottle	sample	title

161

Reviewing Syllable Types and Syllable Boundaries

The goal of all these lessons with syllable types and syllable boundaries is to develop readers and spellers who can effortlessly use these concepts and talk about them readily. The following description of a real lesson with a fourth-grade student should give you an idea of how conversant you want your students to be with the ideas about syllable types and syllable boundaries.

When Nathan and his mother came in for a lesson, he had been studying syllable types, syllable boundaries and multi-syllable rules of spelling for several weeks. His mother said that the homework he'd been doing the night before was confusing and she asked if we could review some of the ideas about syllables.

In order to understand how he was thinking about all of these ideas, the first question that was asked of Nathan was, "What do you remember about syllable types and syllable boundaries?" His answer would demonstrate what he truly understood and what confused him.

His first idea was that if he saw two of the same consonants between two vowels in a word, he should break the syllables between those two consonants. He gave the word "spinner" as an example.

vc/cv

spin/ner

Then he accurately named them twin consonants.

Next, when Nathan was asked what he would do if he had two consonants that were not the same letter between two vowels, he showed he also understood that visual configuration created a syllable boundary between the consonants.

vc/cv

mag/net

The discussion then turned to the question "What kind of consonants have we been dealing with in these two examples—single consonants, consonant digraphs or consonant blends?"

Nathan immediately knew that he had been talking about single consonants, so he was next asked, "What happens if there is a consonant digraph between two vowel letters? Do you separate the syllables between the two consonant letters that make up the digraph as in the word ashen?"

vccv

ashen

Nathan knew that if you break the "s" and the "h" into two different syllables the sound of the digraph changes to /s/ and /h/ instead of /sh/, and he stated that only one "c" should be put above the consonant digraph to represent one sound.

v c v

ashen

This visual configuration VCV was familiar to him and he recalled that the most frequent syllable break for this pattern was V/CV, which made the first syllable an open syllable. He also knew that he had to be flexible with this pattern, moving the syllable boundary after the consonant to make a closed syllable, VC/V. In this word, he decided he had to use the closed syllable pattern.

vc /v

ash/en

Next, Nathan was asked to define a consonant blend, and to explain how it was the same as and different from a consonant digraph. He stated that a consonant blend was made up of two consonant letters that stood for two consonant sounds, and a consonant digraph also has two consonant letters, but only one consonant sound. If we put a consonant blend in a word like *asleep*, the vowel consonant pattern looks like the common VC/CV pattern.

vccv   v/ccv

asleep   a/sleep

Nathan said that consonant blends are not usually broken up, so he thought that the syllable break should come after the first vowel in asleep. He noted that the first syllable is an open syllable with a schwa sound, while the second syllable is a Vowel plus E syllable which begins with a consonant blend.

The idea of morphemes entered our discussion when the word *western* was considered. Because this word is made up of two ideas, two morphemes, the word *west*, which Nathan told me was a compass direction like north, south and east, and the suffix -ern, which means "going in the direction of", deciding on the syllable boundary is complex. If you break the syllables apart based upon meaning, the likely break would be:

vcc/v

west/ern

If you consider how the word sounds when you pronounce it, you would break the word apart between the two consonants.

vc /cv

wes/tern

When Nathan looked this word up in the dictionary, he found that it was acceptable to break the syllables apart both ways.

Nathan was very satisfied when he finished this lesson and felt he understood syllable boundaries. Although almost the entire lesson was spent on this discussion, Nathan was able to remain attentive and engaged, ultimately understanding all of this information.

It is not recommended that you put all this information into one lesson. It would be better to review one or maybe two ideas in a single lesson. To solidify the concepts, practice these skills with games or by dividing gigantic or nonsense words based upon the ideas presented. Be playful as you try to make up silly definitions of any nonsense words based upon prefixes, roots, or suffixes you use to make those words up.

Morphology

Concepts

Words of Anglo-Saxon Origin

Single consonants, consonant blends, single vowels, vowels plus E, and R-controlled vowels, as well as some vowel digraphs and diphthongs are contained in words used in everyday conversations, and they all come to English from the language that the Anglo-Saxon people spoke.

Basic syllable types were present in Anglo-Saxon words, and those early English speakers coined compound words like *earrings, outlaw, toenail,* and *fishhook* to broaden their ability to describe things in their environment.

The short words that describe many common, everyday ideas in the following sentence all come to us from the Anglo-Saxon people:

He still loves his mother, father, brother, sister, wife, son and daughter, lifts his hand to his head, his cup to his mouth, his eye to heaven and his heart to God, hates his foes, likes his friends, kisses his kin and buries his dead, draws his breath, eats his bread, drinks his water, stands his watch, wipes his tears and sheds his blood, and all these things he thinks about and calls good and bad. (Nist, 1966, p. 9)

Anglo-Saxon Compound Words

Anglo-Saxon compound words are made up of two "free" morphemes (which are morphemes that can stand alone) like *earring, homework, blackbird,* and *shoebox.*

Anglo-Saxon Prefixes and Suffixes

To form other words, prefixes that are prepositions were affixed to existing words: *by*stander, *under*stand, *in*side, *out*side. These Anglo-Saxon prefixes and root syllables can also stand alone as separate words.

A common Anglo-Saxon prefix is "a-":

> *a*broad   *a*foot   *a*long

Other common Anglo-Saxon prefixes are "fore-" and "mid-":

> *fore*arm   *mid*line
> *fore*cast   *mid*section

Words with Anglo-Saxon suffixes include:

> alert*ness*   furious*ly*   allow*able*   bear*er*   arm*ful*   frighten*ed*

Inflectional endings, which are Anglo-Saxon morphemes, include suffixes that change tense like "-ed" and "-ing," number and comparatives.

Words of Latin Origin

When the Norman French people invaded and conquered England in 1066 C.E., they brought with them their language, religion and culture.

Today, more than half of the words in English have been derived from Latin-based words. Most of these are multi-syllable words because the structure of Latin-based words is made up of a bound morpheme, a root syllable that cannot stand alone, and a prefix, suffix, or both. Words of Latin origin tend to be more formal and are used in textbooks and writing.

The meaning of Latin-based words is carried in the root syllable, which is modified or changed by the addition of a suffix or prefix. The root syllable "port" means to carry. If we add the prefix "trans-", it means to carry across. If we add the prefix "de-" the meaning of "port" changes, with *deport* meaning to move away from. If we add the suffix "-ation," the word changes from a verb to a noun, *transportation* and *deportation*. Each of these suffixes have a connecting vowel, "i" or "a" to connect the suffix to the base word. Prefixes change the meaning of the root syllable, while suffixes change the part of speech.

Latin Prefixes and Suffixes

Prefixes in Latin-based words give information about number, negation, and time: "bi-" means two, "tri-" means three, "octa-" means eight, "deca-" means ten. "Non-," "un-" and "dis-" are negation prefixes. "Pre-" means before and "post-" means after.

Prefixes also change based upon the letter that begins the root syllable because it sounds better (*euphony*). These prefixes are called *chameleon prefixes* because their spelling changes based upon the initial sound in the root syllable that they are affixed to: *il*logical, *im*moral, *ir*responsible, *im*mobile, and *in*definite.

Some common suffixes are: "-ion," which denotes a noun (*action, partition, accommodation, admission*), "-er" and "-or" which denote a person who does an action (*actor, composer, painter*), and "-ous," which denotes an adjective (*scandalous, ruinous, poisonous, enormous*).

It is valuable to consider how frequently different affixes are used in words. A list compiled by White, Sowell, and Yanagihara (*The Reading Teacher*, 42, p. 306), gives us input on this topic. Their list of twenty prefixes makes up 97% of all prefixed words. Obviously, these are really helpful to teach to our students. The prefixes on this list are: "un-," "re-," "im- in-," "il- ir-," "dis-," "en- em-," "non-," "over-," "mis-," "sub-," "pre-," "inter-," "fore-," "de-," "trans-," "super-," "semi-," "anti-," "mid-," "under-".

On the letter/sound level of Latin-based words, the same consonants that are taught during Anglo-Saxon lessons apply. The most frequent Latin-based vowels are single vowels. There are no vowel digraphs or diphthongs, and as a consequence, Latin-based words have open and closed syllable patterns.

Finally, there are a group of common, irregular ending syllables on the Latin-based level of reading and spelling.

Words of Greek Origin

Words donated to English from Greek are often technical or scientific and are made up of morphemes that do not stand alone. As bound morphemes, these morphemes need to be put together in a word.

Some Greek morphemes are also used as prefixes, with a whole series of words of Greek origin referring to number: "poly-" = many, "uni-" = one, "bi-" = two, "tri-" = three.

Other Greek morphemes refer to size: "mega-" = huge, "micro-" = small or tiny, "demi-" = half.

Here is a list of other Greek morphemes that you will recognize easily:

"archi-" = ancient, old	"crat-" = rule	"geo-" = earth
"photo-" = light	"psych-" = mind	"scope-" = to see, to watch

When you combine the following Greek morphemes, those morphemes signal meaning and part of speech.

"-ology" = the study of, noun	"-y" = noun	"-ture" = noun

Some examples of words of Greek origin would be *architect, architecture, geology, geography,* and *geographic.*

Words of French Origin

There are a number of hints in the spelling of words that derive from French. When the letters "ch" say /sh/ in words, you can be pretty sure that that word was donated to English from French. Some of these words include: *machine, chauffeur, chiffon* and *chalet.*

Another common French spelling pattern is "–ique," which occurs at the end of words: *mystique, antique* and *boutique.*

Many words that have to do with armies, battles, or governance also come from French, including: *battalion, lieutenant, envoy, communiqué, sortie, logistics, détente* and *captain.*

Many names for animals have French origins and include: *lion, dolphin, ferret, giraffe,* and *ostrich.*

Colors also are *beautiful* words of French origin: *turquoise, mauve* and *beige.*

These words are so rich and sound so intriguing. Playing with the pronunciation, looking for spelling patterns that are uniquely French and enlarging our students' vocabulary are all aided by forays into words donated to English by the French language. A variety of such word lists are readily available on the internet.

Activities to Learn Morphemes

1. Use the following "free" morphemes to build as many compound words as you can think of.

grand	shoe	light	play	road	ground
keeper	school	mother	step	child	son
snow	bird	box	father	flash	

2. Build words using root syllables and additional inflectional suffixes, being sure to talk about the multi-syllable orthographic patterns that effect the spelling of words when you add suffixes that begin with vowels.

>   time + *ed*
>
>   timed = drop the *e*
>
>   shape + *s*
>
>   > shapes = no change to the root syllable
>
>   hop + *ing*
>
>   > hopping = doubling rule
>
>   ship + *ment*
>
>   > shipment = no change to the root syllable

Use a root syllable and add prefixes:

>   "rupt-" = to break
>
>   *inter* + rupt
>
>   *e* + rupt
>
>   *dis* + rupt
>
>   *cor* + rupt

Add prefixes and suffixes to a root syllable:

>   *inter* + rupt + *ed*
>
>   *dis* + rupt + *s*
>
>   *cor* + rupt + *ing*

3. Create chained, phonemic awareness exercises by adding, omitting, substituting or shifting whole syllables. Write these morphemes on cards and have the students read the words that you create or have your students spell these word or have the students create their own words.

>   Prefixes: "in-," "non-," "re-," "un-," "mis-"
>   Root syllables: "duct-," "rupt-," "port-"
>   Suffixes: "-s," "-ed," "-ing," "-ment," "-ly"

in duct *ed*	*re* rupt *s*
non duct *ed*	*re* rupt *ly*
non rupt *ed*	*mis* rupt *ly*
non rupt *s*	*mis* port *ly*

4. Break words into their morphemes or count the number of morphemes in words.

> *fixed* = fix + ed = 2 morphemes
>
> *marking* = mark + ing = 2 morphemes
>
> *remarkable* = re + mark + able = 3 morphemes
>
> *outstanding* = out + stand + ing = 3 morphemes
>
> *boys'* = boy + s + ' = 3 morphemes

5. Ask students how the part of speech and/or the meaning of the root syllable changes when you add different suffixes.

> *box* = noun or verb
>
> *boxer* = noun, someone who boxes
>
> *boxes* = plural noun
>
> *boxes* = 2nd person verb, present tense
>
> *boxing* = continual action or an adjective

6. Give students a list of words that have prefixes and/or suffixes, then have them break the words into morphemes and sort the syllables into three categories: prefixes, roots, and suffixes.

7. Present a series of words in a morpheme family, then have your students identify the common root and how each member of the morpheme family is different in meaning and part of speech.

worth	worthless	worthiest
unworthy	worthlessness	worthier

This can also be done with Greek combining forms:

> *ped-* = foot

pedestrian, pedal, peddle, peddler, pedicure, pedometer

> *tele-* = distant

telephone, telegram, telephoto

8. Match prefixes and their meanings:

> *pre-*   not
>
> *un-*   before
>
> *dis-*   again
>
> *re-*   under
>
> *sub-*   wrong

Practical resources to use in the teaching of these ideas to students include:

- *Integrating Morphological Knowledge in Literacy Instruction: Framework and Principles to Guide Special Education Teachers* (Claraval, 2016)
- *Unlocking Literacy, Effective Decoding and Spelling Instruction, 2nd edition* (Henry, 2014)
- *Phonics and Spelling Through Phoneme-Grapheme Mapping* (Grace, 2007)
- *Concept Phonics Worksheets, Level 2* (Fischer, 1997)
- *Resource Masters, Support Materials for LiPS/A.D.D and V/V Programs,* Lindamood-Bell Learning Processes (1993)

Multi-Syllable Orthographic Patterns

Concepts

Multi-syllable Position and Protection Patterns

At the multi-syllable level, there are a number of factors that will influence the pronunciation and spelling of words:

- When suffixes are added to the base word, we need to take into consideration what the last letter/sound in the base word is, as well as its vowel.

- We must identify whether or not the vowel is a single vowel or a vowel team, and if the vowel is a Vowel plus E or if "y" at the end of the base word is preceded by a consonant or is part of a vowel team.

All of these factors will help the learner to discover the *doubling rule*, the *drop the* E *rule*, or the *change the "y" to an "i" rule*.

The past tense and plural patterns are very similar, with the final sound in the base word preceding the suffix determining the sound of the "-ed," "-s" or "-es".

_____

_____

_____

_____

_____

_____

_____

_____

_____

_____

_____

_____

_____

The Doubling Pattern 1-1-1

Concepts

 In order to learn this rule, students must be familiar with the concepts of **weak** and **strong** vowels, the **protection principle**, and the definition of a **syllable**. The doubling rule is considered a multi-syllable rule because when an inflectional suffix is added to one-syllable words, a multi-syllable word often results.

The concept of a **morpheme**, the smallest unit of meaning in a word, has been integrated into this lesson. The word *climb* is one meaning unit, one morpheme, but if an "-er" or an "-ing" is added, its meaning and part of speech significantly changes, with each of these suffixes representing an additional morpheme.

Suffixes are either **inflectional morphemes** that change the tense or number of a word they are attached to, or they will indicate the person (*I, he, she, they, we*). These suffixes do not change the grammatical category of the root word, as in *climb, climbed,* and *climbing,* which are all verbs.

Alternately, a suffix can be a **derivational morpheme** which will change the grammatical function of a root word—*quick* is an adjective, while *quickly* is an adverb.

When adding a suffix to a one-syllable word, the presence or absence of a vowel as the initial letter in the suffix affects the spelling of the root word:

> *pad* + ed = padded

> *sad* + ly = sadly

The spelling change is also dependent upon *the type of vowel* in the root word. If there is a single vowel in the root word, that single vowel will be affected by an **initial** vowel in the suffix.

If there is a digraph or a diphthong vowel—a **strong** vowel in the root word—it will not be affected by the vowel in the suffix:

> weak vowel: *pit* + ed = pitted

> strong vowel: pout + ed = pouted

Further, if the single vowel is followed by one or two consonants, the spelling pattern is different. In order to avoid changing the single vowel sound in the root word, the last consonant in the root word is doubled if the vowel is followed by only one consonant. If the single vowel is followed by more than one consonant, the final consonant is not doubled.

> *pit* + ed = pitted

> *milk* + ed = milked

Teacher – Student Learning Dialogue

Introduction

Many times, letters or syllables are added to the ends of words to change their meaning. Sometimes an "-ed" is stuck on the end of an action word, a verb, to signal that the action happened in the past. Sometimes a suffix such as "-ly" is added to an adjective to change it into an adverb. An "-ing" can be added to a verb to change it into an adjective or a noun (gerund):

jump	sad
jumped	sadly

paint
painting

Suffixes add meaning and information about the part of speech assigned to a word. Spelling is also affected when these meaning-bearing syllables or morphemes are added to root syllables.

Sort this list of suffixes into two groups, those which begin with a vowel letter and those that begin with a consonant:

-able	-ness	-est	-ish
-ful	-er	-y	-or
-ly	-s	-some	-tion
-en	-es	-ship	-ation

The spelling of some root words will be affected by these suffixes:

mad + en = madden	*milk* + y = milky	*spill* + ed = spilled
mad + er = madder	*milk* + ed = milked	*spill* + s = spills
mad + est = maddest	*milk* + s = milks	*spill* + ing = spilling
mad+ly = madly		

- The first question to ask when figuring out this pattern will be, "Is this base word a one-syllable word?" All the base words on this list are one-syllable words.

- Secondly, we must also determine whether the vowel in each word is weak or strong.

Using the words in this list, mark the words with weak vowels with a W and the words with strong vowels with an S:

mad + en = madden	*mad* + est - maddest	*mad* + er = madder
W	W	W
milk + y = milky	*milk* + ed = milked	*milk* + s = milks
W	W	W
spill + ed = spilled	*spill* + s = spills	*spill* + ing = spilling
W	W	W

All of these words have weak vowels so the spelling variation must involve more than the vowel in the base word.

- Does the spelling of the base word change when a suffix is added to it that begins with a consonant like "-ly" or "-s"? *No*
- How many consonants follow each weak vowel in each word, one or two? *Either one or two*
- With words that have weak vowels followed by only one consonant, if a suffix that begins with another vowel is added to that word, will that vowel affect the vowel in the base word? *Yes, it will make the weak vowel say its letter name:*

  mad + en = maden   *mad* + er = mader   *mad* + est = madest

- How can that weak vowel be "protected" or prevented from changing its sound? Will another consonant protect it or another vowel? *If I add another consonant the first vowel will be protected. If I add a vowel, I will change the sound in the root word*
- In words that have a weak vowel followed by two consonants, do I need to double the last consonant to protect the weak vowel? *No, milk + ed = milked; spill + ing = spilling*

You can see that when there is a weak vowel in the base word that is followed by only one consonant, when adding a suffix that begins with a vowel, the last consonant in the base words needs to be doubled to protect the weak vowel.

If there is a weak vowel in the base word with two consonants following it, it is already protected by those consonants and we don't have to double any letters in the base word.

If there is a weak vowel in the base word with one consonant following it and the suffix that is being added begins with a consonant, the last consonant in the base word and the first consonant in the suffix protect the weak vowel and no letter is doubled in the base word.

When a base word has a strong vowel, it is not affected by the suffix beginning with a vowel or a consonant and the spelling of the base word is not changed.

Here is a set of four questions to ask yourself as you think through this doubling pattern:

- Is this a one-syllable word?
- Does this base word have a weak, single vowel?
- Is the vowel followed by one consonant letter?
- Does the suffix that begin with a vowel?

If the answer is "yes" to all the questions above, double the last consonant in the base word to protect the weak vowel.

Let's look at some other words and see if the last consonant in the root word needs to be doubled to protect the vowel. In each case, ask the four questions that will aid in making your decision to double or not.

aim + **ing**

1. Is this a one-syllable word? *Yes*
2. Does this base word have a weak single vowel? *No*
3. Is the vowel followed by one consonant letter? *Yes*
4. Does the suffix begin with a vowel? *Yes*

The last consonant in the base word does not have to be doubled because the vowel is strong: *aiming*

jump + **ed**

1. Is this a one-syllable word? *Yes*
2. Does this base word have a weak single vowel? Yes
3. Is the vowel followed by one consonant letter? *No*
4. Does the suffix begin with a vowel? *Yes*

The last consonant in the base word does not have to be doubled because there are two consonants that follow the single vowel, which is enough protection: *jumped*

red + **ness**

1. Is this a one-syllable word? *Yes*
2. Does this base word have a weak single vowel? *Yes*
3. Is the vowel followed by one consonant letter? *Yes*
4. Does the suffix begin with a vowel? *No*

The last consonant in the base word does not have to be doubled because the suffix begins with a consonant. There are two consonants between the vowels and that is enough protection: *redness*

hit + **ing**

1. Is this a one-syllable word? *Yes*
2. Does this base word have a weak single vowel? *Yes*
3. Is the vowel followed by one consonant letter? *Yes*
4. Does the suffix begin with a vowel? *Yes*

The last consonant in the base word has to be doubled to protect the weak vowel: *hitting*

Here is a list of words and the suffixes to be added to the root words. Use the four questions to decide if the ending consonants in the root words have to be doubled to protect the vowel in the root word:

red + en	*miss* + ing	*fit* + ful	*spoon* + ed	*sit* + ing
coin + ed	*sad* + ness	*bat* + er	*count* + er	*run* + er

(Answers: *redden, missing, fitful, spooned, sitting, coined, sadness, batter, counter, runner*)

This spelling pattern can be summarized by saying: When you have a one-syllable word with a one-letter weak vowel followed by one consonant sound, and you are adding a suffix that begins with a vowel, *double the last consonant in the root word to protect the weak vowel.* **If any of these conditions are not present in the root word or the suffix, you do not have to double the last consonant in the root word.**

The questions used in this lesson can be used as a step card for the doubling rule. If the answer is "yes" to all of the questions, double the last consonant to protect the weak vowel. If the answer is "no" to any of the questions, do not double the last consonant when adding a suffix.

Past Tense

Concepts

The past tense inflectional ending involves not only a spelling pattern, but also morpheme units (a unit of meaning within a word). When the letters "-ed" are added to a verb, the spelling and pronunciation of the word are changed, as well as giving information about when the action took place.

There are two morphemes in the word, *looked*. One unit of meaning is the action described by the base word and the second unit of meaning is the inflectional ending "-ed". The sounds represented by "-ed" change based upon the letter which immediately precedes the "-ed" in the base word and whether that sound is voiced or unvoiced.

It is essential to explore both the meaning and the spelling changes with your students.

Historically, there were two classes of verbs in English: *strong verbs* and *weak verbs* (not to be confused with the terms *strong vowels* and *weak vowels* that are used in this book). The markers for past tense for the class of strong verbs was a shift in the vowel: *fly / flew, see / saw*, or *run / ran*.

The marker for the class of weak verbs was the "-ed" inflectional ending. It is helpful to explain some of this historic information to students who often are upset by the perceived exceptions to spelling patterns that appear random.

Because the inflectional ending "-ed" begins with a vowel, rules that interact with the *past tense rule*—including the *doubling rule,* the *drop the E rule,* the *multi-syllable doubling rule,* and the *changing "y" to "i" rule*—affect the spelling of words. Each of these rules will be taught in subsequent lessons. Select the words that you use for the lessons based upon which of these spelling patterns have been taught to your students.

Furthermore, because this morphological spelling pattern has many ideas, you may choose to do several introductory lessons—reviewing weak and strong vowels, the doubling rule, and then exploring when "-ed" sounds like /t/ or /d/, and finally when "-ed" sounds like /id/ in two or three lessons.

Your students also need to know the concepts of root words or base syllables, suffixes, and inflectional and derivational endings.

Inflectional endings are suffixes that add meaning to the word, but do not affect the grammatical function of the base word. "-Ed" is an inflectional ending when it turns a present tense verb into a past tense verb – wash, washed.

Derivational endings are suffixes that add meaning to the word, and do affect the grammatical function of the base word. When you add "-ed" to a verb it can act as an adjective, as in "painted chest". In this phrase, "painted chest", -ed is acting as a derivational suffix.

Teacher – Student Learning Dialogue

Introduction

We have talked about root words or base words and suffixes. They each have roles as meaning units or morphemes. In this lesson, we are going to investigate the past tense morpheme.

Can you define Root Words? Suffixes? Morphemes?

What does "past tense" mean? What does "present tense" mean?

Elicit real life examples of present and past tense verbs from your students first by giving examples and having the students label the verbs as past or present tense. Then ask the students to generate examples of their own.

There are two ways to linguistically note verbs that are in the past tense. Some verbs change the vowel spelling to indicate time, like the verbs *grow/grew*, *see/saw* or *swim/swam*. Most past tense verbs add the morpheme "-ed".

Let's explore some verbs and see how the past tense pattern operates. I will read these verbs and ask you to tell me how I would say that the action happened yesterday.

Today I jump, yesterday I ... ? *Jumped*

Proceed through this list with your students, using the sentence stem and writing the correct spelling after each word. Discuss the doubling rule where applicable and the vowel shift where applicable.

jump/jumped	run/ran	walk/walked	throw/threw	bag/bagged
play/played	sit/sat	talk/talked	pitch/pitched	catch/caught
glow/glowed	sing/sang	look/looked	plan/planned	warn/warned

What sound(s) do the "-ed" letters represent in each of these words?

jumped /t/	walked /t/	cooked /t/
played /d/	talked /t/	pitched /t/
strolled /d/	fished /t/	looked /t/
planned /d/	warned /d/	glowed /d/

How will you, as a speller or reader, know which sound the past tense marker "-ed" makes? There has to be a pattern here.

When we studied the consonants, what was the linguistic relationship between the letters "t" and "d"? *These two letters are formed the same way in the mouth, "d' is voiced and "t" is unvoiced, they are consonant partners.*

We also know that the letters that follow one another in words often have a sound and spelling relationship. Let's identify which letters precede the past tense marker when it sounds voiced, /d/, and which letters precede the past tense "-ed" when it's unvoiced, /t/.

/d/	/t/
ay, n, ow	p, k, ch

Label these consonants and vowels based upon whether they are voiced or unvoiced:

/d/	/t/
ay, n, ow	p, k, ch
All of these are voiced	All of these are unvoiced

Do you see a pattern here? When the last letter in the base word is voiced, the past tense marker "-ed" sounds like the voiced /d/; when the last letter in the base word is unvoiced, the past tense marker "-ed" sounds like the unvoiced /t/.

Let's look at these words and pay attention to the sounds at the end of the root words.

- What is the last sound in each of these root words? /t/, /d/
- Which of these sounds is voiced? Unvoiced?

pad	start
voiced	unvoiced

If we apply the sound pattern that we discovered in other words in this lesson to these words, we should add a voiced /d/ to the word "pad" and we should add an unvoiced /t/ to the word "start".

If I add a /d/ to the word "pad", would there be a new sound added to the word? Would the past tense marker be heard in the word "pad"? *No*

If I add a /t/ to the word "start", would there be a new sound added to the word? Would the past tense marker be heard? *No*

To be able to distinctly hear the past tense marker in words that end in a "t" or a "d," we add a vowel sound /i/ to the past tense marker and the "-ed" sounds like /id/.

padded	started
/paddid/	/startid/

These words now are two-syllable words because of the added vowel sound.

Here are some words to practice this part of the past tense rule with:

scold	hunt	plant	land	paint	rest	melt
twist	fold	hand	dust	end	bond	need

A step card created with your students and written in their own words is a very effective reminder for pronunciation of past tense morphemes.

When I see the past tense marker "-ed" added to word, I have to ask myself these questions:

- What is the last letter in this root word?

- Is the last letter in the root word voiced or unvoiced, the letter "t" or "d"?

- If the last letter is "t" or "d" the "-ed" says /id/.

- If the last letter is not "t" or "d" and it is unvoiced, the "-ed" says /t/.

- If the last letter is not "t" or "d" and it is voiced, the "-ed" says /d/.

A curious problem arises because of the sound of the "-ed" morpheme. When a person spells a word, they have to decide whether to use "t," "d," or "-ed".

The way to figure this out is to ask yourself:

"What is the meaning of this word? Is this a base word, a word which has the added /t/ or /d/ sounds to indicate that the action occurred in the past, or is the base word a single morpheme, a single meaning unit that I cannot subtract the /t/ or /d/ from? If I take the /t/ or /d/ sound off the base word, does it have a recognizable meaning?"

The meaning and context in which words are used will help students understand which spelling to use. Here are a few words to explore these concepts with:

missed - mist	passed – past	based – baste	allowed - aloud
find – fined	band – banned	gored – gourd	rode – rowed

_____

_____

_____

_____

_____

_____

_____

_____

_____

Plurals

Concepts

 When exploring this multi-syllable rule, keep in mind that the plurals spelling pattern also involves the concept of morpheme units, which are units of meaning within words.

When you make a noun plural, you are dealing with two morphemes: the meaning of the base word, the noun, and the fact that it is greater than one, plural. If you have the word *girl*, it represents one morpheme. When you add an "-s" to the end of the word, it indicates that there is more than one girl, and *girls* now represents two morphemes. When teaching this spelling pattern to students, be sure to incorporate both the spelling ideas, as well as the concept of morphemes.

There are a number of ways we can indicate when a noun is plural in English, with the most common being the addition of an "-s" or an "-es" to the word. Some nouns change their spelling without the addition of an "s" (*man/men, woman/women, child/children*), other nouns will change the spelling of the base word (*shelf/shelves, elf/elves*).

Another parallel idea is the fact that we use "-s" and "-es" attached to verbs—*she smiles, he runs, she pushes, it branches, John brags*—with the sound relationships being the same for these verbs as the sound relationships for nouns.

It is suggested, however, that you not teach all of these aspects of the plural and verb morphemes at once, but rather create multiple lessons that can last up to a week each in order for students to have time to stabilize each aspect of the pattern before receiving new information.

Teacher – Student Learning Dialogue

Introduction

 *Ask your students what they already know about the concept of plurals. If they are confused about the meaning, and/or cannot give examples of the concept, proceed with the following dialogue.*

If I have a bag and want to indicate that I have more than one bag, I use a specific sound marker to communicate the idea of a plural noun and either add "-s" or "-es" to the end of the word.

The word "bag" has three letters that denote the single idea of a "container". If I add the letter "-s" to bag, that single letter adds another idea—the fact that I have more than one bag, which is now a plural rather than a singular noun.

In this lesson we want to figure out how to pronounce these plural morphemes and when to add on an "-s" or an "-es" to form a plural noun.

Let's make the following words plural by adding "-s".

| boy | wall | truck | bat | booth | bag | table | chair |
| top | mark | pool | bath | pot | palm | seat | car |

What sound does the "-s" represent in each of these nouns when it is added?

boys /z/	bags /z/	pools /z/
wall /z/	tables /z/	baths /s/
tracks /s/	chairs /z/	palms /z/
bats /s/	tops/s/	seats /s/
booths /z/	marks /s/	cars /z/

The "-s" either says /s/ or /z/

How will you as a speller or reader predict which sound the plural "-s" makes? There has to be a pattern here.

- When we studied the consonants, what was the linguistic relationship between the letters "s" and "z"? *They are a consonant pair because they are formed the same way in the mouth, the "z" is voiced, and the "s" unvoiced*

We also know that letters which follow one another often have a sound and spelling relationship. Let's identify which letters precede the plural marker "-s," and whether they are voiced or unvoiced.

/s/	/z/
"t," "p," "k," "th"	"oy," "g," "m," "l"
all of these are unvoiced	all of these are voiced

Do you see a pattern here?

When the last letter in the base noun is unvoiced, the plural "-s" marker sounds liked the unvoiced /s/. When the last letter in the base noun is voiced, the plural "-s" marker sounds like the voiced /z/.

What about the "-es" spelling for the plural marker? Let's label the words that have "-es" as the plural marker based upon whether the last letter in the word is voiced or unvoiced:

| charges | boxes | bushes | badges | churches |

charge, badge = voiced

church, box, bush, bus = unvoiced

If we apply the sound pattern that we discovered in the other words in this lesson, we should add an unvoiced /s/ to all of the words which end with an unvoiced consonant, and we should add a voiced /z/ to all of the words which end in a voiced consonant.

- **If I add an /s/ to the word "bush" or "box" would the plural marker be heard?** *No*

- **If I added a /z/ to the word "charge" would the plural marker be heard?** *No*

To be able to distinctly hear the plural marker on words which end in an "s," "z," "sh," "ch," "x" or /j/, we add the plural marker "-es," which sounds like /iz/.

A vowel sound is added to the /z/ to distinctly hear the ending consonant on the root word, as well as the plural morpheme. Adding this vowel sound to the plural "-es" changes the original one-syllable word into a two-syllable word.

An excellent resource for the other spellings of plurals is *How to Teach Spelling*, by Laura Toby Rudginshky and Elizabeth C. Haskell, Educators Publishing Services (epsbooks.com).

Step cards are very helpful for students to use for remembering how to pronounce the plural morpheme. Here is one possible card for reference, but it is only an example, as it is much better to create a step card with students and to encourage them to write it in their own words.

> **When I want to add the plural markers "-es" or "-s" to a word, I have to ask myself:**
>
> - **What is the last letter in the root word, "s" or "z", "ch," "x," or "ge"?**
> - **If the last letter is "s" or "z", "ch," "x," or "ge," add the "-es" which says /iz/.**
> - **If the last letter is any other letter, and it is unvoiced, add an "-s," which says /s/.**
> - **If the last letter is any other letter, and it is voiced, add the "-s" which says /z/.**

To teach the verb plus "-s" or "-es," follow the exact sequence of questions, applying them to verbs from a list like this one:

print	sing	stroll	snag	change
push	drop	trot	paint	box
snow	walk	gallop	cook	punch
fix	hop	sew	sip	see

Isn't it interesting that many of the words on this list could be either nouns or verbs? The only way to know how to name the part of speech of a word is to use that word in a sentence to determine if it is functioning as a noun or a verb!

He hit two home runs = *noun*

He runs five miles = *verb*

Adding Suffixes to Multi-Syllable Words Ending in "E"

Concepts

 When adding a suffix to a word, the presence or absence of a vowel as the suffix's initial letter affects the spelling of the root word when the vowel in the root word has a Vowel plus E.

use + ing = using

use + er = user

When the root word has a Vowel plus E (*nice, pole, use*) and a suffix is being added that begins with a vowel ("-er," "-est," "-ing," "-able") the "e" in the root word is dropped before the suffix is added.

When the suffix begins with a consonant, ("-ment," "-ly," "-ness") and the root word has a Vowel plus E, the "e" in the root word is not dropped before the suffix is added.

state + ment = statement

late + ness = lateness

The *notable exception* to this pattern is when the "e" in the root word acts as a marker for another spelling pattern as in:

peaceable = the "e" is signaling the "c" to say /s/

vengeance = the "e" is signaling the "g" to say /j/

Teacher – Student Learning Dialogue

 ### Introduction

We have learned that the spelling of root words and suffixes are closely related. The sound of the past tense suffix "-ed" and the plurals "-s /-es" are tied to the last sound in the base word. In this lesson, we will be looking at another interaction between a root word and other suffixes.

place + ing = placing	*place* + ment = placement
late + er = later	*late* + ness = lateness
create + or = creator	*create* + ed = created
create + ing = creating	*create* + ation = creation
use + ing = using	*use* + ful = useful

In this lesson, we are adding suffixes which begin with either a vowel or a consonant. When we add a suffix to the root word whose vowel is a Vowel plus E, the "e" at the end of the root word is sometimes dropped.

In other words, when we add the suffix to a root word whose vowel is a Vowel plus E, the "e" at the end of the root word is not dropped.

Knowing there has to be a pattern to the different spellings, we want to be able to know when to drop the "e" and when not to drop the "e".

Sort these words into two categories, one that has suffixes beginning with a vowel letter, the other with suffixes that begin with a consonant letter.

Beginning with Vowels	Beginning with Consonants
late + er = later	*late* + ness = lateness
create + or = creator	*use* + ful = useful
create + ed = created	*place* + ment = placement
create + ing = creating	*spite* + ful = spiteful
space + ing = spacing	*tire* + some = tiresome
use + ing = using	

Do you see a pattern?

- What happens to the "e" at the end of root word when the suffix begins with a vowel? *The "e" is dropped before the suffix is added*
- What happens to the "e" at the end of the root word when the suffix begins with a consonant? *The "e" is not dropped before these suffixes*

Be careful with words like "changeable" and "peaceable" where the "e" is doing the job of making the "g" say /j/ and the "c" say /s/. In these two words, the "e" is changing the sound of the "c" or the "g".

Step card for Drop the E rule:

> **If a base word has a Vowel plus E, and a suffix is being added to the base word, ask yourself:**
>
> - **What type of letter does the suffix begin with, a consonant or a vowel?**
>
> **If the base word has a Vowel plus E, and the suffix begins with a vowel letter, take the "e" off the base word and add the suffix.**
>
> **If the base word has a Vowel plus E, and the suffix begins with a consonant letter, add the suffix to the base word without removing the "e".**

Students should read, spell, and write phrases and sentences with words that have these suffixes added to base words, explaining the meaning and part of speech of the base word and how it is changed by adding the suffix.

You can work with base words and add suffixes, or you can work with the affixed words and ask your students to parse out the morphemes:

use + ing = using

spite + ful = spiteful

using = use + ing

spiteful = spite + ful

_____

_____

_____

_____

_____

_____

_____

_____

_____

_____

_____

_____

_____

_____

_____

_____

_____

_____

_____

_____

Adding Suffixes to Multi-syllable Words Ending in "Y"

Concepts

 In order to learn this spelling/reading pattern students must understand that "Y" can act as part of diphthongs and digraphs ("oy," "ay," "ey") or as a single grapheme. They should also know both the Position Principle and the Protection Principle.

When "y" acts as a vowel at the end of a word, it sounds like /ie/ or /ee/ and is preceded by a consonant. When "y" is part of a digraph or a diphthong, it is a part of a vowel team ("ay," "oy," "ey").

When adding any suffix, the single letter "y" preceded by a consonant, the "y" will change to an "i" before adding the suffix, unless that suffix begins with the letter "i". In English, you cannot have two letters "i" next to each other.

try + ed = tried

try + ing = trying (not triing)

When adding any suffix to a vowel that teams with "y" ("oy," "ay," or "ey") do not change the "y" because it is a part of the vowel team.

stay + ed = stayed

annoy + ing = annoying

Teacher – Student Learning Dialogue

Introduction

When "y" acts as a vowel at the end of a word it can stand alone, as in "fly" or "carry". "Y" can also be a part of a vowel team, as in "stay," "coy," and "money".

When suffixes are added to words that have "y" as a final letter, the "y" behaves differently. Sometimes it changes to an "i" and sometimes not. Let's see if you can figure out this spelling pattern!

Part 1: Words Ending with "Y" Preceded by a Consonant

carry, carrying, carried, carries

spy, spying, spied, spies

try, trying, tried, tries

- What letters come before "y" in these groups of words, a consonant or a vowel?
  A consonant

- When "-ing" is added to the words "carrying," "spying," and "trying," does the "y" change? *No*
- When "-ed" or "-es" is added to the words "carried," "cried," and "tried," does the "y" change? *Yes*

There has to be a reason for this difference. When English books were first being published, the people who did the typesetting decided that having the letter "i" two times in a row would be confusing for readers, who might mistake them for a "u," so they decided that when adding the suffix "-ing" to a base word ending in "y" preceded by a consonant, they would not change the "y" to an "i".

When adding other suffixes to a base word ending in "y" with a consonant preceding it, the "y" was changed to an "i" before adding suffixes that do not begin with an "i".

Here is a graphic that summarizes this spelling/reading pattern:

Consonant + "y" + <u>i</u>ng = -ying
Spying

Consonant + "y" + all other suffixes = "y" changes to "i" + suffix
Spies, spied

Let's use the some of the following words to practice this pattern:

fly	ply	pry	shy	sky	spy
creepy	grouchy	needy	bumpy	handy	misty
sty	baby	fifty	tidy	taffy	bunny
ugly	curly	rusty	jumpy	oily	plenty
puppy	county	penny	daisy	ivory	enemy
candy	army	city	copy	body	bully
deny	supply	deny	glorify	reply	imply

Add the following suffixes to the base words on the board:

-ing	-es	-er	-ful	-s
-ed	-ly	-est	-ment	

When doing exercises like this, it is important to expand your students' perspective beyond mechanically spelling each word.

Some of the words in this list are nouns, some are verbs and each suffix has a meaning and signals a part of speech. Ask students to sort the words based upon what part of speech the words represent when suffixes are added to the base word.

Further, when your students add suffixes to some of the base words in this exercise, some real words and some nonsense words will result. Ask the students in a different lesson to sort the words based upon whether the affixed words are real words or nonsense words.

Suffixes indicating parts of speech of base words:

Nouns	Verbs	Adjectives	Adverbs
"-s," "-es,"	"-s," "-es"	"-er," "-est"	"-ly"
"-ment"	"-ed"	"-ful"	
"-ing"	"-ing"	"-ing" "-ly"	

Changing the suffixes changes the part of speech:

Nouns	Verbs	Adjectives	Adverbs
flies	flying	grouchy	grouchily
armies	denies	bodily	shyly
	denied		

Part 2: Words Ending in "Y" Preceded by a Vowel

toy	toying	toyed	toys
play	playing	played	plays
key	keying	keyed	keys

- **What letters come before "y" in these groups of words, a consonant or a vowel?** *Vowels "o," "a," and "e"*
- **Did the vowel teams "oy," "ay" or "ey" change when suffixes were added?** *No*

When "y" is part of a vowel team it is not changed to an "i", no matter what the type of letter the suffix that is added to the base word begins with, a vowel or consonant. The letters in a vowel teams can't be changed.

Here is a graphic that summarizes this spelling/reading pattern:

____ Vowel + "y" + suffix
Playing, plays, played

The vowel + "y" does not change when adding suffixes.

Words to practice this pattern with:

spray	day	pay	clay	tray	stray
sway	driveway	delay	subway	highway	relay
display	chimney	volley	monkey	turkey	kidney
toy	decoy	employ	stay	cloy	ploy

Add the following suffixes to these base words:

-ing   -ed   -es   -ly   -er   -est   -ful   -ment

Some of the words are nouns, some are verbs, some are adjectives or adverbs. Which combinations of base words and suffixes are real words? Nonsense words?

Ask your students to read, spell, and write phrases and sentences with the words that have the suffixes added to base words, being sure to always have them explain the meaning and part of speech of the base word and how it is changed by adding the suffix.

You can work with base words and add suffixes, or you can work with the affixed words and ask students to parse out the morphemes:

volley + ing = volleying

displayed = display + ed

A board game that practices adding these inflectional suffixes to base words can help to provide ample practice that is engaging.

You can create a game board with a variety of base words arranged on a four by four matrix and use a pair of dice upon which you write different suffixes on each face of the die.

After a student rolls the dice and drops it on the game board, they have to connect the base word and the suffix on the dice face using the *doubling rule*, the *past tense* or *plural rule, the drop the E rule*, or the *change the "y" to an "i" rule.* If the constructed word is a real word, the player earns two points. If the affixed word is a nonsense word, the player only earns one point.

Make a tool bar for the rules that you are reviewing so students can refer to it to help them recall and work thoughtfully with the different rules. The game can also be modified by having fewer suffixes written on the dice.

The Multi-Syllable Doubling Pattern

Concepts

The multi-syllable doubling rule shares many concepts with the single syllable doubling rule. The multi-syllable pattern focuses on the last syllable of a multi-syllable word.

In order to decide whether to double the last consonant in a multi-syllable when adding a suffix, the following questions need to be answered:

- After identifying the vowel in the last syllable, determine whether that vowel is a weak single vowel or a strong vowel.
- If the vowel is a weak single vowel, is it followed by one or two consonants?
- Is the last syllable in this multi-syllable word accented?
- Does the suffix that you are adding to the root word begin with a consonant or a vowel?

The question that distinguishes the multi-syllable doubling pattern from the one-syllable doubling pattern involves the accent pattern in the word. If the final syllable in the root word is accented, and if the vowel in that syllable is a weak single vowel followed by only one consonant, when adding a suffix that begins with a vowel the last consonant in the multi-syllable root word is doubled to protect that weak single vowel.

$$\text{com - pel}' + \text{ing} = \text{compelling}$$

If any of these conditions is not met, the last letter in the root word should not be doubled.

$$\text{suf}'\text{- fer} + \text{ing} = \text{suffering}$$

Teacher – Student Learning Dialogue

Introduction

We have already learned the one-syllable doubling rule. In this lesson, we will see how to add suffixes to a multi-syllable word, and apply the doubling rule to those words.

When working with a multi-syllable word, we change the questions to:

1. Is this a multi-syllable word?
2. Is the last syllable accented?
3. Is there a weak single vowel in that last syllable?
4. Is there one or more than one consonant following the weak vowel in the last syllable?
5. Am I adding a suffix that begins with a vowel?

If the answer is, "yes", to all these questions, double the consonant in the last syllable before adding the suffix.

As you practice determining if the last syllable in the root word is accented or not, some of the ideas we learned about accent and the sound of the vowel will help.

The vowel in an accented syllable says the sound you expect not /u/ or /i/, the schwa sounds. The accented syllable is said longer than the unaccented syllable. The accented syllable is also louder than the unaccented syllable.

One way of determining whether a syllable is accented or not is to pay attention to the vowel and whether it is saying its expected sound. Another way to determine whether a syllable is accented is to hum the word and listen for the louder syllable that is hummed for a longer time.

Let's use these words to determine which syllable is accented:

admit	forgot	pilot	perform	deliver	defend
contain	forbid	transmit	subtract	limit	gather

ad-mit´	for-got´	pi´ lot	per-form´	de-liv´-er	de´fend
con-tain´	for-bid´	trans-mit´	sub-tract´	lim´-it	ga´ther

Once we have determined whether the last syllable is accented, we can ask the other questions.

admit + ing

1. Is this a multi-syllable word? *Yes*
2. Is the last syllable in this word accented? *Yes*
3. Does that last syllable have a weak single vowel? *Yes*
4. Is the weak single vowel followed by one consonant letter? *Yes*
5. Am I adding a suffix which begins with a vowel? *Yes*

The answer is "yes" to all of these questions, so double the last consonant in this multi-syllable word to protect the weak vowel. *Admitting*

pilot + ed

1. Is this a multi-syllable word? *Yes*
2. Is the last syllable in this word accented? *No*
3. Does that last syllable have a weak single Vowel? *Yes*
4. Is the weak single vowel followed by one consonant letter? *Yes*
5. Am I adding a suffix which begins with a vowel? *Yes*

The answer is not "yes" to all of these questions, so do not double the last consonant in this multi-syllable word to protect the weak vowel because the first syllable is accented. *Piloted*

deliver + ing

1. Is this a multi-syllable word? *Yes*

2. Is the last syllable in this word accented? *No*

3. Does that last syllable have a weak single vowel? *No, it is an R-controlled vowel*

4. Is the weak single vowel followed by one consonant letter? *No*

5. Am I adding a suffix which begins with a vowel? *Yes*

The answer is not "yes" to all of these questions, so do not double the last consonant in this multi-syllable word to protect the strong vowel. *Delivering*

contain + ed

1. Is this a multi-syllable word? *Yes*

2. Is the last syllable in this word accented? *Yes*

3. Does that last syllable have a weak single vowel? *No, it has a vowel digraph*

4. Is the weak single vowel followed by one consonant letter? *No*

5. Am I adding a suffix which begins with a vowel? *Yes*

The answer is not "yes" to all of these questions, so do not double the last consonant in this multi-syllable word to protect the strong vowel. *Contained*

defend + ed

1. Is this a multi-syllable word? *Yes*

2. Is the last syllable in this word accented? *Yes*

3. Does that last syllable have a weak single vowel? *Yes*

4. Is the weak single vowel followed by one consonant letter? *No*

5. Am I adding a suffix which begins with a vowel? *Yes*

The answer is not "yes" to all of these questions, so do not double the last consonant in the multi-syllable word to protect the weak vowel because there are two consonants following it. *Defended*

Proceed through the rest of the words in this lesson using these questions.

This spelling pattern can be explained with the following summary:

When you have a multi-syllable word, if the last syllable in the word is accented, there is a weak single vowel in that syllable followed by one consonant sound and you are adding a suffix that begins with a vowel, *double the last consonant in the root word to protect the weak vowel.* If any of these conditions are not present in the root word or the suffix, you do not have to double the last consonant in the root word.

The questions asked in this lesson can also be used as a step card for the multi-syllable doubling rule.

Morpheme Families

Concept

 After students have learned the multi-syllable protection rules, as well as how to read and spell the past tense and plurals patterns and other inflectional endings, it is time to strongly bridge the relationship between spelling, grammatical categories and meaning. Because English is truly based in sound/letter associations, orthographic patterns, and meaningful units or morphology, it is considered to be a morphophonemic language.

A meaningful sortie into this arena could focus on exploring how the meaning and function of a root word changes when different inflectional and derivational suffixes are added to it. Consider introducing one or two morpheme families (a root word and its different inflectional and derivational suffixes) each week to accomplish this.

The following exercises demonstrate how to build morpheme families by taking a root word and adding several inflectional and derivational suffixes to it. This helpful list of common suffixes includes the parts of speech they signal:

"-ing" = adjective, verb	"-ive" = adjective
"-ish" = adjective	"-ist" = noun
"-ous" = adjective	"-er", "-est" = comparative adjectives
"-ly" = adverb	"-er" and "-or" = noun, a person who
"-tion" = noun	"-ity" = noun, a concept
"-sion" = noun	"-ian" = noun, a person
"-an" = noun, a person	"-al" = adjective

Discuss the difference in meaning and usage with your students as the different affixes are added to the root syllable, then have them use the words in both oral and written sentences.

tailor	nerve	play	critic
tailors	nerves	plays	critics
tailored	nervous	played	criticize
tailoring	nervously	player(s)	criticism
		playing	criticizing

Other activities can include Latin prefixes, suffixes and roots. Practicing with morpheme families will help students understand information when writing, spelling, and reading.

One practical strategy is to begin teaching a few prefixes and a root syllable in combination with inflectional and derivational suffixes that your students already know. You can also have your students make their own personal sets of affixes that they have learned to use when building multi-syllable morpheme families.

Using the following prefixes, root syllables and suffixes, have your students create as many words as they can think of. You can put the prefixes, base syllables and suffixes on cards and the students manipulate the cards to produce as many words as possible. The suffixes in the following lists are a mixture of Anglo-Saxon inflectional endings and Latin prefixes and suffixes.

Root Syllables
"port-," "spect-," "duct-"

Prefixes
"de-," "in-," "un-," "dis-," "trans-," "re-," "ex-," "ab-," "ad-"

Suffixes
"-ion," "-ation," "-or," "-er," "-s," "-es," "-ing," "-ed"

Possible Answers

deport	inspect	aqueduct
airport	inspection	conduct
deportation	inspector	educated
deported	prospect	introducing
export	prospector	reduce
import	respect	reduction
transport	prospecting	deduct
transportation	spectator	abduction
porter	spectacles	abductor
transporting	inspected	educated

Common, Irregular Ending Syllables

When working with the Latin layer of words, students will benefit by learning about *common, irregular ending* syllables:

- The term *common* tells us that these syllables are at the end of many words.

- Being *irregular*, the vowels and some of the consonants at the beginning of these ending syllables, do not say their expected sounds. The vowel in these final syllables are often muffled, the schwa sound. The syllable before the common irregular ending syllable can be a connective vowel ("a," "i," or "u").

- The term *ending* indicates these syllables are suffixes.

In order to learn about these common, irregular ending syllables, students need to have a working knowledge of the following definitions and concepts:

- A *syllable* is a word or a part of a word that has one and only one vowel sound.

- An *accented syllable*, which is said louder than an unaccented syllable, has a clear vowel which sounds the way you expect it to.

- The vowel in an *unaccented syllable* is muffled into a schwa.

- A *suffix* is a syllable that comes at the end of a base or root word. It is a bound morpheme which must be attached to a base or root syllable or word. The suffix changes the tense, number, person and part of speech of the base word.

- A key question to ask when identifying the grammatical function of words with these common, irregular ending syllables is whether or not the base word plus the ending syllable is a noun, a verb, an adjective or an adverb.

When presenting these common irregular ending syllables to students, offer only one or two patterns at a time.

When you present words with common, irregular endings, be sure to:

- Discuss how many syllables there are in the word and how many morphemes it contains.

- Examine the kinds of syllables the word has.

- Identify which syllable is accented and which is unaccented.

- Zero in on the fact that these ending syllables are unaccented and have a vowel that has been muffled into a schwa sound.

- Analyze the consonants in last syllable, demonstrating that the consonants in this syllable often do not have their expected sound, while being sure to note if there is a connective vowel before the suffix.

One of the most useful, common, irregular ending syllables is "-ion," which when affixed to a base word can have several pronunciations and regular spelling patterns:

- "-tion" (also with connectives "-ition" and "-ation"): *action, mention, attention, fiction, fraction, variation, migration, inspiration, organization, revolution, collection, addition, position*

- "-cion" and "-cian": *magician, clinician, pediatrician, electrician, musician politician, physician, coercion, suspicion*

- "-sion" and "-sian": *occasion, invasion, precision, television, pension, expression, permission, artisian, Parisian*

- "-gion" and "-gian": *Belgian, theologian, Norwegian, legion, religion, region*

Helpful ideas to use when teaching students about these common, irregular ending syllables include:

- Irregular ending syllables that all say /shun/: "-tion," "-tian," "-cian," "-cion," "-sion," and "-sian".

- The most common spelling of the common, irregular ending syllable that says /shun/ is "–tion".

- Endings which usually indicate words that name a person: "-tian," "-cian," and "-sian" (*Alsatian, magician, Asian*).

- Endings which usually indicate words that name objects or ideas: "-tion," "-cion," "-sion" (*action, coercion, provision*).

- Endings which can be pronounced /shu/ or /zhu/, /shun/ or /zhun/ are: "-sia," "-sian," "-sion" (*possession, Russian, evasion, Asian, Asia*).

- The last consonant in the base word will provide a hint as to which spelling of the common, irregular ending you choose to spell /shun/: *act - action, magic - magician, possess - possession.*

- If there is a connecting vowel before the common irregular ending syllable /shun/, use the "-tion" spelling: rend*i*tion, add*i*tion, applic*a*tion, impos*i*tion, inhal*a*tion.

Practice which uses varied tasks helps students integrate the concepts and spellings of these syllables:

- Having them say a common irregular ending syllable, then identify it in an array of several common, irregular ending syllables.

- Having them spell the common, irregular ending syllables.

- Having them read words with these common, irregular ending syllables.

- Playing and creating games with words that have common, irregular ending syllables.

- Dictating words, phrases, and sentences with words that have common, irregular ending syllables.

As your students master the spelling and reading of a few of these suffixes, you can then introduce two or three more.

This may seem like a lot of work for one overarching concept, common, irregular ending syllables, however, knowing these common, irregular ending syllables will open up the reading and spelling of thousands of multi-syllable words that students need to know in middle school and beyond.

Glossary of Linguistic Terms

Affixes – Syllables that are glued to a root word - prefixes or suffixes which change the root word's meaning and part of speech. Ex. *part* = a noun or a verb, *de*part = to leave, *partial* = an adjective, *partially* = an adverb.

Alphabetic Principle - the concept that a spoken sound is portrayed by one or more letters in a written word.

Auditory Discrimination – The ability to hear the difference between two sounds. Some sounds are more easily judged than others. Consonant pairs and consonants that share the same type of air production, continuals and sibilants, and some vowels are challenging. Easy discriminations include /t-f/, /o-oo/. Challenging discriminations include /f-th/, /s-sh/, /i-e/.

Base Word – Root Syllable – A base word is a word that has meaning on its own, a free morpheme. A root syllable usually cannot be used independent of its affixes and it carries the primary meaning of the word. Prefixes and suffixes can be added to both a base word and a root syllable to change its meaning and part of speech. *Build* = base word, *rebuild* = prefix + base word, *rebuilding* = prefix +base word + suffix, *struct* = bound root syllable, *construct* = prefix + root syllable, *construction* = prefix + root syllable + suffix.

Closed Phonemes – Consonants are defined as closed phonemes because some part of the mouth, the lips or tongue, restrict the flow of air to produce the sound.

Consonant Blends and Clusters – Two or three consonants that occur one right after the other, with no intervening vowels which represent two or three phonemes or sounds. Initial blends are seen at the beginning of a word or syllable and final blends are seen at the end of a word or syllable. Initial blends = bl-, cr-, st-, pr-. Final blends = -ct, -mp. Consonant Clusters = str-, spl-, squ-.

Derivational Suffixes – A suffix that changes the grammatical category of the base word or root word it is attached to. *act* = verb - *action* = noun, *envy* = noun - *envious* = adjective, *enormou*s = adjective - *enormously* = adverb.

Digraphs - Two consonant or vowel letters that say one sound which is different than the sounds produced by the individual letters in the digraph. /sh/ is different than /s/, /h/. /oi/ is different than /o/, /i/.

Diphthongs – Two vowel letters that say one sound which is different than the sounds produced by the individual letters in the diphthong. A diphthong is produced in the mouth by gliding the lips, tongue and jaw from one position to another. "Oi,oy", "ou,ow".

Etymology – the study of word origins and the evolution of words' meaning, pronunciation and spelling over time.

Flexibility Principle - A spelling principle that states that when spelling or reading a word in English, there may be multiple pronunciations of the letters and their sounds, as well as many spelling patterns to represent those sounds. A reader or speller's thinking must therefore include deciding what the possible and probable sound/letter relationships are. Examples: "Ea" can say /ee/, /e/, or /ae/ as in the words *each, breath* and *break.* The most common sound of "ea" is /ee/, the least common sound of "ea" is /ae/.

Grapheme – A letter or combination of letters that represent one speech sound or phoneme. "E", "ea", "eau", "eigh" are all graphemes.

High Frequency Words – Words that appear very frequently in texts which have one or two sound/letter pairings that do not follow the expected spelling patterns. These words often have evolved over time, being adopted from other languages. An Anglo-Saxon example is the word, knight. We no longer pronounce the /k/ and the /gh/ as they were originally pronounced. For students to learn these words thoughtfully, they should use their phonemic awareness skills, as well as mapping skills, noting which letters do not "play fair". Investigating the meaning of the word and its etymological roots also helps to understand the evolution of the pronunciation and spelling of the word.

Inflectional Suffixes – A suffix which is added to base word or root syllable that changes its number, (plurals), cat – cats, tense, (past tense), jump – jumped or person, (switching from first person to third person), he sits – they sit.

Markers – Letters that signal changes in sound and spelling patterns of surrounding letters. Examples include the C rule and the Vowel Plus E rule or the GE-DGE rule.

Morphemes – the smallest unit of meaning, a word or an affix. In the word, **girls'** , there are three morphemes – girl, -s and the possessive apostrophe.

Onset - The consonant letter(s) that precede the vowel in the word. TAKE, **SN**AKE, **THR**ILL.

Open Phonemes – Vowels are defined as open phonemes because the lips, tongue and jaw are open when articulating the vowel sound.

Orthography – The writing system of a language, the correct and acceptable sequences of letters that represent the sounds in the word, its unique spelling patterns.

Phoneme – The smallest unit of sound produced in speech than can be combined with other phonemes to form words.

Phonemic Awareness – The ability to hear the differences between sounds, auditory discrimination, the ability to locate where a sound is within a word, phoneme isolation, the ability to pull a word apart into its component sounds, segmenting, the ability to push individual sounds together to form a word, blending, the ability to add or omit a sound within a word and the ability to move sounds around within the word, shifting sounds. These skills are fundamental to reading and spelling words thoughtfully.

Phonological Awareness – The ability to hear whole sentences and to break those sentences into words, the ability segment a word into syllables and/or onset and rime.

Position Principle - The idea that the spelling of a sound within a word is dependent either on where it is on a word or syllable, the beginning, middle or end and that spelling pattern is dependent on the letters that surround it. For example, the letter "Y" acts as a consonant in the beginning of a word or syllable and as a vowel in the middle and end of a word or syllable.

When a "C" is followed by the letters, "i, e, y" is sounds like /s/. When "C" is followed by any other consonant or vowel it says /k/.

Prefix – a syllable that can be added to the end of a base word or a root syllable . That syllable changes the meaning root or base word it is affixed to, read, *pre*read, *mis*read.

Protection Principle - If there is a weak, one letter vowel in a word or final syllable and you want to maintain the sound of that single vowel, you spell ending sounds with spelling patterns of more than one consonant letter: sack – sake, pill – pile, catch – pooch.

Rime - In a one syllable word, the vowel and consonants which follow the vowel.

Schwa – When a vowel is in an unaccented syllable in a function word or multi-syllable word, the vowel is muffled and said quickly and the sound of the vowel is /u/ or /i/ instead of the common pronunciation of that vowel: th**e**, **a**bout, divisi**o**n.

Single Consonants and Vowels – Single letters that represent one phoneme: a, b, t, i.

Sound/Symbol Correspondences – the paired association between sounds or phonemes and the written letters or graphemes.

Strong Vowels - Vowel digraphs or diphthongs, two letter graphemes, that have stable sounds that are not influenced by the consonants or vowels that follow them.

Suffix - A syllable that is added to the end of a base word or root syllable that changes its tense, number or part of speech: skip- skip**s**, port – port**able.**

Syllable - A word or a part of a word that has one and only one vowel sound. Syllables may have consonants before and/or after that vowel: I, my, am, stand.

Syllable boundaries - The points at which syllables within a word are divided. Because each syllable can have one and only one vowel sound, a multi-syllable word is comprised of multiple syllables. Syllable boundary patterns can be V/V, V/CV, VC/V, VC/CV.

Weak Vowels – Single vowels are highly susceptible to the influence of letters that follow them, their sounds change. If an R sits immediately after a single vowel, that single vowel changes its sound. If -nk or -ld come after a single vowel, the sound of the single vowel changes, -ink, -ild.

References and Resources

Adams, Marilyn Jager. *Beginning to Read.* Cambridge, MA: The MIT Press, 1990.

Anderson, Lorin W. & David R. Karthwhol. *A Taxonomy of Learning, Teaching and Assessing, A Revision of Bloom's Taxonomy of Educational Objectives.* Longman, 2001.

Archer, A., & Hughes, C. *Explicit instruction: Effective and Efficient Teaching.* New York: Guilford Press, 2011.

Aumann, Maureen. *Step Up to Writing.* Sopris West, 2009.

Balmuth, Miriam Ph. D. *The Roots of Phonics: A Historical Introduction.* Baltimore, MD: York Press, 1982.

Bear, D., Invemizzi, M., Templeton, S., & Johnston, F. *Words Their Way: Word study for Phonics, Vocabulary and Spelling Instruction* (2nd Edition). Upper Saddle River, NJ: Merrill of Prentice Hall, 2000.

Beck, Isabel, Margaret G. McKeown, Linda Kucan. *Bringing Words to Life, Robust Vocabulary Instruction.* The Guilford Press, 2013.

Berninger, Virginia W., Katherine Vaughan, Robert D. Abbott, Allison Brooks, Kristin Begay, Gerald Curtin, Kristina Byrd, and Steve Graham. *Language-Based Spelling Instruction: Teaching Children to Make Multiple Connections Between Spoken and Written Words.* Learning Disability Quarterly, 23 (2000): 117–35.

Bishop, Margaret M. *The ABC's and All Their Tricks: The Complete Reference Book of Phonics and Spelling.* Milford, MI: Mort Media, Inc, 1986.

Blevins, Wiley. *Phonics from A to Z.* New York, NY: Scholastic Professional Books, 1998.

Bowen, Carolyn C. *Angling for Words: A Study Book for Language Training.* Novato, CA: Academic Therapy Publications, 1972.

Calfee, R. C., Baldwin, L. S., Chambliss, M., Curley, R., Henry, M., Munson R., et. al. *Components of Reading Instruction.* Stanford, CA: Unpublished manuscript, Stanford University,1984.

Ebbers, Susan M. MA. Ed. *Vocabulary Through Morphemes: Suffixes, Prefixes, and Roots for Intermediate Grades.* Longmont, CO: Sopris West, 2004.

Farrell, L., et al. *The Simple View of Reading.* The Center for Development and Learning Blog, February 1, 2010 (www.cdl.org/articles/the-simple-view-of-reading/).

Fisher, Phyllis. *Concept Phonics, Worksheets, Level 2.* Oxford Publishing, 1997.

Fitzpatrick, Jo. *Phonemic Awareness: Playing with Sounds to Strengthen Beginning Reading Skills* (K. Hall Edition). Cypress, CA: Creative Teaching Press, Inc, 1977.

Grace, Kathryn E. S. *Phonics and Spelling Through Phoneme-Grapheme Mapping.* Longmont, CO: Sopris West, 2007.

Kearns, Devin M and V.vM. Whaley. *Helping Students with Dyslexia Read Long Words: Using Syllables and Morphemes.* Teaching Exceptional Children, Vol. 51, Issue 3 (2019): 212-225.

Kilpatrick, D. A. *Essentials of Assessing, Preventing, and Overcoming Reading Difficulties.* Hoboken NJ: Wiley, 2015.

Kilpatrick, D. A. *Equipped for Reading Success, A Comprehensive, Step-by-Step Program for Developing Phonemic Awareness and Fluent Word Recognition.* Syracuse, New York: Casey & Kirsch Publishers, 2016.

Hanna, Paul, Jean S. Hanna, Richard E. Hodges, and Edwin H. Rudorf, Jr. *Phoneme-Grapheme Correspondences as Cues to Spelling Improvement.* Washington, DC: US Department of Education Publication No. 32008, U.S. Government Printing Office, 1966.

Henry, Marcia. *Unlocking Literacy: Effective Decoding and Spelling Instruction.* Baltimore, MD: Paul H. Brookes, 2003.

Johnson, Kristin and Polly Bayrd. *Megawords, Decoding, Spelling and Understanding Multisyllable Words.* Toronto: School Specialty, Inc, 2010.

Langeberg, Donald N. et. al. *Report of the National Reading Panel; Teaching Children to Read: An Evidence-Based Assessment of the Scientific Research Literature on Reading and Its Implications for Reading Instruction.* U. S. Department of Health and Human Services. National Institute of Child Health and Human Development: National Institute of Health, Washington, DC: U.S. Government Printing Office, 1999.

Levine, Mel MD. *Educational Care: A System for Understanding and Helping Children with Learning Problems at Home and in School.* Educational Publishing Service, 2002.

Lindamood, P., & Lindamood, P. *The Lindamood Phoneme Sequencing Program for Reading, Spelling, and Speech, Examiner's Manual.* Austin, TX: Pro-Ed, 2011.

Lindamood-Bell Learning Processes. *Resource Masters, Support Materials for LiPS/ A.D.D. and V/V Programs.* Gander Educational Publishing, 1993.

Linnea, C. Ehri. *The Development of Spelling Knowledge and Its Role in Reading Acquisition and Reading Disability.* Journal of Learning Disabilities, Vol 22, #1 (1989): *356–65.*

Linnea, C. Ehri. *Learning to Read and Learning to Spell, Two Sides of a Coin.* Topics in Language Disorders (2009): 19-49.

Linnea, C. Ehri. *Learning to Read and Learning to Spell Are One and the Same, Almost. Learning to Spell: Research, Theory, and Practice across Languages,* ed. Charles A. Perfetti, Laurence Rieben, and Michel Fayol. Mahwah, NJ: Lawrence Erlbaum Associates, (1997): 237–69.

Lovett, M. W., Frijters, J. C., Wolf, M., Steinbach, K. A., Sevcik, R. A., Morris, R. D. *Early intervention for children at risk for reading disabilities: The impact of grade at intervention and individual differences on intervention outcomes.* Journal of Educational Psychology, 109, (2017): 889–914.

Malatesha, R. Joshi, Rebecca Treiman, Suzanne Carreker, and Louisa C. Moats. *How Words Cast Their Spell: Spelling is an Integral Part of Learning the Language, Not a Matter of Memorization.* American Educator, Winter 2008-2009.

Moats, Louisa C. *Speech to Print: Language Essentials for Teachers.* Baltimore, MD: Paul H. Brookes, 2014.

Moats, Louisa C. *How Spelling Supports Reading.* American Educator, 2005-2006.

Moats, Louisa C. *Teaching Reading is Rocket Science, 2020. What Expert Teachers of Reading Should Know and Be Able to Do.* American Federation of Teachers, 2020.

Perfetti, C. A. *The Universal Grammar of Reading.* Scientific Studies of Reading (2003): 7, 3–24.

The Reading League. *Decodable Text Sources.* (www.thereadingleague.org/wp-content/uploads/2019/08/Decodable-Text-Sources-updated-August-2019.pdf.) 2020.

Rudginsky, L. T., Haskell, E. C. *How To Spell Series, Books 1-4.* Cambridge, MA: Educators Publishing Services, 1993.

Rudginsky, L. T., Haskell E. C. *How to Teach Spelling.* Cambridge, MA: Educators Publishing Services, 1985.

Scarborough, H.S. *Connecting early language and literacy to later reading (dis)abilities: Evidence, theory, and practice.* In S. Neuman & D. Dickinson (Eds.) Handbook for Research in Early Literacy (97–110). New York, NY: Guilford Press, 2001.

Seidenberg, Mark. *Language at the Speed of Sight: How We Read, Why So Many Can't, and What Can Be Done About It.* Basic Books, New York, 2017.

Shaywitz, Sally MD. *Overcoming Dyslexia: A New and Complete Science-Based Program for Reading Problems at Any Level.* New York, NY: Alfred A. Knopf, 2003.

Spear-Swerling, Louise. *Structured Literacy and Typical Literacy Practices: Understanding the Differences to Create Instructional Opportunities for Teaching* Exceptional Children, Vol. XX, No. X, (2018): 1-11.

The Reading League, May 1, 2020. *Decodable Text Sources.* (www.thereadingleague.org/wp-content/uploads/2019/08/Decodable-Text-Sources-updated-August-2019.pdf)

Taft, M. *Lexical access via an orthographic code: The basic orthographic syllabic structure (BOSS).* Journal of Verbal Learning and Verbal Behavior (1979): 18, 21–39.

Torgesen, J. K. *Recent Discoveries from Research on Remedial Interventions for Children with Dyslexia.* In M. Snowling & C. Hulme (Eds.). *The Science of Reading: A Handbook* (521–537). Oxford, UK: Blackwell, 2006).

Treiman, Rebecca. *Beginning to Spell.* New York: Oxford University Press,1993.

Washburn, Kevin D. *The Architecture of Learning, Designing Instruction for the Learning Brain.* Washburn Clerestory Press, 2010.

White, T. G., Sowell, J., Yanagihara, A. *Teaching elementary students to use word part clues.* The Reading Teacher (1989): *42,* 302-308.

Appendices

APPENDIX A

Spelling Review Schedule

Student Name:

T = Taught   N = Needs more practice

Simple One Syllable Level

Single Consonants and Vowels

Consonant Digraphs

Consonant Blends

Vowel Patterns

Vowel + E

R-controlled Vowels

Au, aw

Ou, ow

Oi, oy

OO

Two Vowel Friends

Ai, Ay

Oa, Ow

Ea, Ey, Y

-Awn, -Awl, -Owl, -Own

Kind Old Pink Things

Sophisticated Consonant Patterns

C

G

Y

X

QU

One Syllable Protection Patterns

Weak & Strong Vowels

FLoSS

k/ck

ch/tch

ge/dge

Syllable Types

Define Syllables & Schwa

Closed

Open

Vowel + E

Vowel Teams

R-controlled

Consonant LE

Multi-Syllable Spelling Patterns

Past Tense

Plurals

Doubling

Drop the E

Change the Y to I

Multi-Syllable Doubling

Common, Irregular Ending Syllables

APPENDIX B

Letter/Sound Relationships

p	b	t	d
k	g	f	v
th	s	z	sh
ch	j	m	n
ng	w	wh	h
l	r	c	x
y	qu	a	e
i	o	u	oo
ae	ee	ie	oe
ue	oi	oy	ou
ow	ir	er	ur
ar	or	igh	

Teacher Recording Sheet for Letter/Sound Relationships

p	b	t	d
—	—	—	—
k	g	f	v
—	—	—	—
th	s	z	sh
—	—	—	—
ch	j	m	n
—	—	—	—
ng	w	wh	h
—	—	—	—
l	r	c	x
—	—	—	—
y	qu	a	e
—	—	—	—
i	o	u	oo
—	—	—	—
ae	ee	ie	oe
—	—	—	—
ue	oi	oy	ou
—	—	—	—
ow	ir	er	ur
—	—	—	—
ar	or	igh	
—	—	—	

APPENDIX C

Consonant & Vowel Bingo

P	B	T	D
K	G	A	E
I	O	U	F
V	TH	<u>TH</u>	H
A	E	I	O
U	WH	W	P
B	T	D	K

Consonant & Vowel Bingo Template

APPENDIX D

Connect 4 in a Row

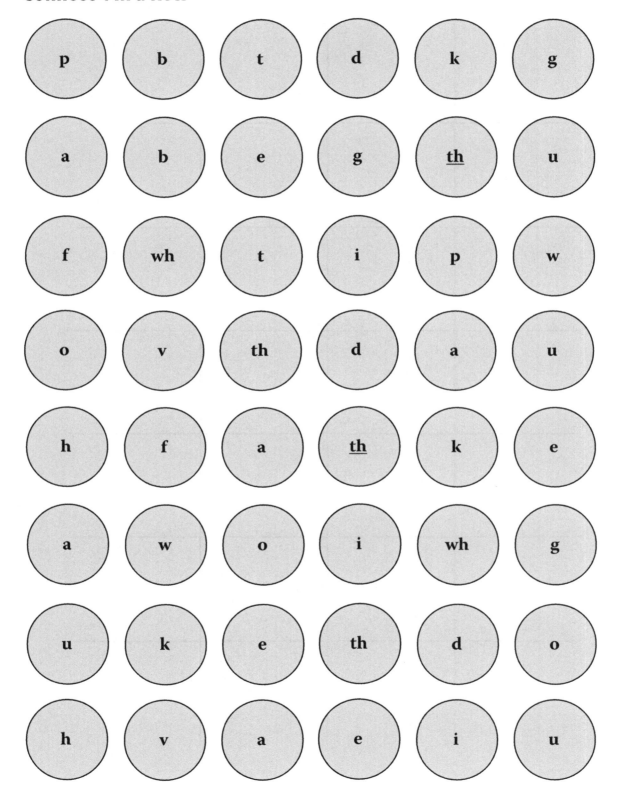

Part V

APPENDIX E

Checker Pieces

APPENDIX F

Decodable Texts

Young Readers: Grades K-2

Bob Books

Simple Words Decodable Chapter Books

Don on a Log Books

Voyager Sopris Supercharged Readers

Dr. Maggie's Phonic Readers

EPS Phonics Plus Readers

For All Ages

Flyleaf Emergent Readers

All About Reading

Half Pint Readers

Flyleaf Decodable Literature Library

High Noon Dandelion Launchers

Go Phonics Readers

InitiaLit Readers from MultiLit (AUS)

Junior Learning Decodable Readers

Jolly Phonics (US & UK)

PhonicBooks (UK)

Junior Learning Decodable Readers

Piper Books (UK)

Little Learners Love Literacy (AUS)

Turning Pages (UK & AUS)

Miss Rhonda's Readers

SLANT System Readers

Primary Phonics Storybook Sets

Spalding Readers

SPELL-Links Reading Library

S.P.I.R.E. Decodable Readers

Pocket Rockets (AUS)

SuperBooks

Superkids

95% Group Decodable Passages

Voyager Sopris Power Readers

Teens & Adults: Grades 3-8

High Noon Fantasy Series

High Noon Moon Dog Series

High Noon Sound Out Chapter Books

High Noon Sound Out Nonfiction Series

Best for Older Readers

Teen & Adult Phonics (TAP) Library

Saddleback TERL Phonics Book Sets

Made in the USA
Las Vegas, NV
10 July 2023